The Thorpe Committal

This book describes the proceedings at Minehead magistrates' court, when Jeremy Thorpe and three others were committed for trial. The defence case has not been heard, and the authors and publishers do not imply that any allegations made in court whatsoever, whether against the defendants or against any other person mentioned, are true. The magistrates merely decided that the Crown have presented a case to answer: Jeremy Thorpe and his co-defendants 'might be convicted by a reasonably-minded jury, properly directed' on the prosecution case presented. Of course, no part of the defence case was before the magistrates at all.

The Thorpe Committal

Peter Chippindale and David Leigh

ARROW BOOKS

Acknowledgements

The authors would like to thank Irene and Jane at Sidekicks for typing the manuscript so efficiently, and Pat and Jeannie for their tolerance.

London
January 1979

Arrow Books Limited
3 Fitzroy Square, London W1P 6JD

An imprint of the Hutchinson Publishing Group

London Melbourne Sydney Auckland
Wellington Johannesburg and agencies
throughout the world

First published 1979

© Peter Chippindale and David Leigh 1979

Made and printed in Great Britain
by The Anchor Press Ltd
Tiptree, Essex
ISBN 0 09 920400 2

Contents

Plan of Minehead court-room		6
The characters		8
Chronology of events as alleged by the Crown		10
Preface		12
1	The Crown	13
2	Bessell	26
3	Bessell cross-examined	46
4	Hayward and Dinshaw	67
5	Andrew Gino Newton	84
6	Norman Scott	102
7	Scott cross-examined	116
8	Miller and others	130
9	The police	144
10	'The prosecution must have been desperate'	160
11	A case to answer	176

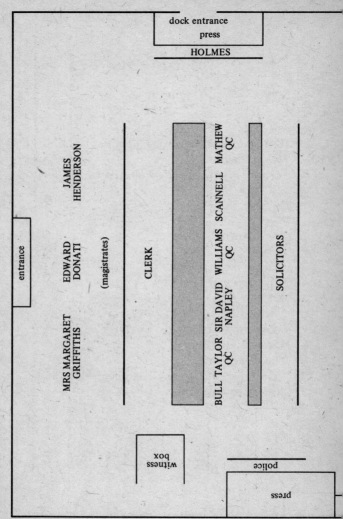

36 feet

dock entrance
press

HOLMES

JAMES HENDERSON

EDWARD DONATI

(magistrates)

MRS MARGARET GRIFFITHS

entrance

CLERK

BULL TAYLOR QC

SIR DAVID NAPLEY

WILLIAMS

SCANNELL

MATHEW QC

SOLICITORS

witness box

police

press

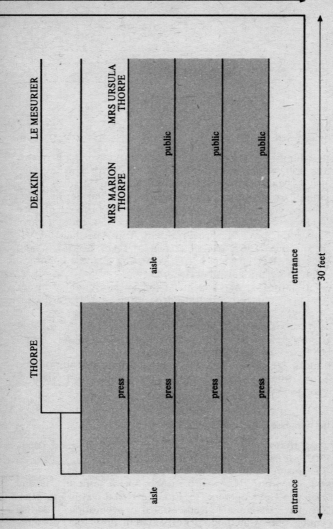

Plan of Minehead court-room

THORPE

DEAKIN   LE MESURIER

MRS MARION THORPE   MRS URSULA THORPE

press   public

press   public

press   public

press   public

aisle   aisle

entrance   entrance

30 feet

The characters

The accused

JOHN JEREMY THORPE, 49. Privy Counsellor and Leader of the Liberal Party 1967-76. MP for North Devon since 1959; Chairman United Nations Association since 1976. Son of Conservative MP for Rusholme, Manchester. Education: Eton; Trinity College, Oxford. President Oxford Union 1951. Barrister, Inner Temple, 1954. Liberal Party Treasurer 1965-7; Vice-President Anti-Apartheid Movement since 1969. Married (twice). Lives in Devon and London. Recreations: music, collecting Chinese ceramics. Member, National Liberal Club.

DAVID HOLMES, 48. Tax and financial consultant. Former Deputy Treasurer, Liberal Party. Education: Oxford University. Single. Lives in Manchester and London.

JOHN LE MESURIER, 46. Head of Pyle Carpet Discount Centre, Pyle. Married. Lives at St Brides Major, South Glamorgan. Recreation: gardening.

GEORGE DEAKIN, 38, amusement machine distributor and club owner. Married. Lives at Port Talbot, West Glamorgan.

The witnesses

PETER JOSEPH BESSELL, 57. Liberal MP for Bodmin 1964-70. Married (twice). Businessman (retired). Lives at Oceanside, California, USA.

JACK ARNOLD HAYWARD, OBE, 55. Chairman, Grand Bahama Development Co. Ltd. Married. Lives in Freeport, Grand Bahama. Recreations: promoting British endeavours, watching cricket, amateur dramatics, preserving the British landscape, and keeping all things bright, beautiful and British.

8

NADIR DINSHAW. Accountant. Born Karachi. Lives in Jersey.

ANDREW GINO NEWTON, 32, former airline pilot (British Island Airways). Education: Chiswick Polytechnic. Lives in Chiswick, London.

NORMAN SCOTT (b. Josiffe, known as Lianche-Josiffe), 38. Education: Bexleyheath secondary modern. Divorced. Schools horses; sometime male model. Lives in North Devon.

DAVID MILLER, 32. Education: Chiswick Polytechnic. Silk-screen printer. Lives in Cardiff.

MICHAEL CHALLES. Detective Chief Superintendent, Avon and Somerset Police. 26 years a policeman. Based at Central Police Station, Bristol.

Persons mentioned

BARRIE PENROSE and ROGER COURTIOUR, former BBC television journalists. Authors of *The Pencourt File* (1978).

DAVID ENNALS, 56. Secretary of State for Social Services since 1976. MP for Norwich North. Minister of State, DHSS, 1968-70.

LORD GOODMAN (formerly Arnold Goodman), 65. Solicitor and public official. Partner Goodman, Derrick. Education: Downing College, Cambridge. Chairman Arts Council 1965-72. Chairman Housing Corporation 1973-7. Chairman Newspaper Publishers' Association 1970-6. Master of University College, Oxford since 1976.

DAVID STEEL, 44. Leader of Liberal Party since 1976, MP for Roxburgh, Selkirk and Peebles since 1965.

LORD STOW HILL (formerly Sir Frank Soskice), 76. Home Secretary 1964-5. Labour MP for Newport, Mon., 1956-66. Died 2 January 1979.

Chronology of events as alleged by the Crown

1959
October   Thorpe elected MP for North Devon
1961
November   Scott meets Thorpe at House of Commons. They have homosexual relations at Thorpe's mother's house
Christmas   Scott stays in Devon with the Colliers
1962
New Year   Scott has homosexual relations with Thorpe in Devon after the 'Broomhills lunch'
19 December   Scott makes homosexual allegations to police
1963
February   Scott loses Swiss luggage
1965
Spring   Thorpe confides to Bessell. Scott writes 'Dublin letter'
April   Thorpe and Bessell have 'Ritz lunch'
1967
January   Thorpe elected Leader of the Liberal Party
August   Bessell starts paying weekly 'retainer' to Scott
1968
December   Thorpe proposes Scott's death to Bessell
1969
January   Thorpe incites Holmes to kill Scott
13 May   Scott marries
August   Scott rings Bessell about his Insurance card
1970
May   Hayward donates £150,000 to the Liberal Party
18 June   General Election. [Thorpe's majority 369]
October   Scott's wife starts divorce proceedings
1971
January   Bessell and Holmes pretend to lure Scott to USA
May   Liberals investigate Scott's claims
10 June   Scott makes second police statement
1972
March   Scott's lover, Gwen Parry-Jones, commits suicide

4 May   Scott makes outburst against Thorpe at her inquest
21 December   Scott divorced
1974
January   Bessell 'disappears' in USA
27 February   Holmes pays £2500 for Scott's letters
28 February   General Election. [Thorpe's majority 11,072]
10 April   Thorpe asks Hayward to send him £10,000
3 May   Hayward sends cheque to Jersey
10 October   General Election. [Thorpe's majority 6721]
November   Scott's 'Dublin letter' passed to Thorpe by
  Mirror
28 November   Thorpe tells Hayward Liberals £17,000 short
1975
4 February   Holmes and Deakin steal photo and letters from
  Scott at Imperial Hotel, Barnstaple
26 February   Newton introduced at Showman's dinner
5 March   Thorpe asks Hayward to send another £100,000
Spring   Dinshaw starts to hand over cash to Holmes
6 July   Thorpe tells Hayward the £10,000 less urgent
24 October   Newton shoots Scott's dog, Rinka
18 November   Newton interviewed by original police inquiry
24 November   Hayward sends the £10,000 to Dinshaw
1976
19 January   Holmes sees Bessell, who writes 'Barnes letter'
29 January   Scott makes outburst against Thorpe in court
2 February   Thorpe makes 'Isaac Foot' confession to Bessell
5 March   Holmes admits he paid £2500 for letters
14 March   Thorpe calls Scott a liar in *Sunday Times*
19 March   Newton convicted on firearms charge. Jailed
10 May   Thorpe resigns as Liberal Leader
1977
6 April   Newton released from jail
18 April   Newton given £5000 cash by Le Mesurier
27 October   Thorpe calls press conference
10 November   Thorpe asks Dinshaw to lie about money
1978
4 April   Thorpe asks Hayward to threaten Bessell
13 and 18 April   Thorpe threatens Dinshaw
4 August   Thorpe, Holmes, Deakin and Le Mesurier charged
20 November   Committal hearing opens at Minehead
13 December   Thorpe, Holmes, Deakin and Le Mesurier
  committed for trial at the Old Bailey. All deny charges

Preface

No book like this has ever before been published in Britain. Previous books have always been published after a trial and the jury's verdict. But the Thorpe case is no ordinary matter. Millions of people in this country and all over the world are already arguing fiercely about it. Few of them understand this *cause célebre*, despite the huge newspaper coverage.

The four defendants exercised their right under the law to make the prosecution lay out its evidence against them in a full-scale committal hearing. The defence exercised its further right to lift reporting restrictions, so that both the evidence and the cross-examination of witnesses could be made public. The magistrates had to decide whether there was a case to answer. They ruled that there was. The defence will produce its own witnesses for the first time at the trial, when a jury will decide whether the four men are guilty or innocent. They all deny the charges.

This book describes an extraordinary three weeks in a public court-room, under the due and respected process of British justice. As Sir David Napley, Mr Thorpe's solicitor, wrote, after the Minehead committal: 'All judicial processes should be undertaken, both for the protection of the individual accused and the public generally, in the full glare of publicity. I still believe, with Edmund Burke, that where mystery begins, justice ends.'

1

The Crown

Hard by the bleak expanse of Exmoor, on the 1000-foot cliff-tops fronting the Bristol Channel, there is an unremarkable, rough lay-by off the A39 trunk road. Here, on a wild October night in 1975, a Great Dane called Rinka died by a single bullet to the head. Her owner was left terrified by the roadside. The reason for the shooting seemed at first as obscure as the spot where it took place.

But that event set in motion investigations ranging over seventeen years, and culminating in the formal charging of the Rt Hon. John Jeremy Thorpe, Privy Counsellor, former Leader of the Liberal Party and still MP for North Devon. He was accused of the most serious crimes ever to be laid against a British politician.

On Monday 20 November 1978 – over three years later – Thorpe put on his familiar brown trilby and drove his white Rover 3500 with its distinctive DUO number-plate into the small seaside town of Minehead, to fight the charges. As an indirect result of one pistol shot he was facing two counts – conspiracy to murder and incitement to murder. Both carry a life sentence.

The proceedings took place automatically in the unlikely setting of Minehead, Somerset. Under English law any charge, no matter how serious, has to be heard initially in the local magistrates' court. The dog had died just inside the border with Devon – six miles away up steep Porlock Hill. Normally the local Bench dispatches major cases to a higher court in minutes. Lists of witnesses and exhibits are handed in under a paper

13

procedure which lawyers know as a Section One Committal. None of the evidence is given, and the defendant waits until trial to contest the prosecution case.

Thorpe had chosen to do things differently. He had exercised his option to have a full Section Seven committal. This procedure was used in every case until 1967, when the Criminal Justice Act introduced Section One committals to save time and money. But any defendant who wishes can still use the old procedure to force the prosecution to lay out its full case. The defendant's lawyer does not reveal the defence case, but is allowed to cross-examine the prosecution witnesses as much as he likes. He then submits that the case against his client is so weak that it is not fit to put before a jury. The magistrates – if they agree – have the power to dismiss the case immediately. Otherwise they decide there is a case to answer and commit it to a higher court for jury trial. In 1977, according to Home Office statistics, fewer than 3 per cent of people charged with serious offences had their cases thrown out at committal in this way.

By adopting this course, Thorpe had also unintentionally fulfilled the promise of every local parliamentary candidate – to bring prosperity to the West Country. Minehead, which closed its Butlin's Holiday Camp at the end of the season and went into its normal winter slumber, had been invaded that weekend by the world's media. They had poured into the town, erecting television gantries and arc lights opposite the court entrance, and filling the bar of Sir Charles Forte's Beach Hotel to overflowing. Extra supplies were being ordered.

The press were in a mixed mood that morning as they waited outside court and saw Thorpe's Rover rounding the bend to a cry of, 'Here he comes!' The photographers, barred from the court itself, were happy enough as they admired the rainbows on a glorious Somerset morning. They knew their blurred pictures of faces snatched through car windows would appear in the papers, whatever happened. But the journalists felt frustrated. They were certain they would listen to sensational and bizarre allegations. But none would be published. The 1967 Act severely restricts the reporting of committal proceedings unless the defence specifically asks for publicity. The reporters had checked with the lawyers and resigned themselves to the restrictions staying down. Their reports would have to be confined to the charges, and the names and ages of the defendants, plus what 'colour' they could find in the scene outside. Even a detailed description of the defendants' clothing is forbidden.

Some reporters were already at work by 9 a.m., interviewing the queue for the public gallery – headed by a retired stone-mason, Harry Broadley. He was prudently clutching a spare set of batteries for his hearing aid. Other writers noted that the court, with commendable efficiency, shared the building with Minehead's police station, where Thorpe, with three others, had been charged on a warm August day three months previously. The solid red-brick building with its Georgian-style windows is set back from the main road amongst middle-class semis on the outskirts of town, they put in their notebooks. Despite its modern appearance, it had been opened in 1939 by Herbert Morrison.

Gagged as they thought they would be, nevertheless 140 journalists and would-be authors had applied for the 32 seats allocated to them in the public gallery, which they would share with the first 21 ordinary people in the queue. There had been so much demand for press seats that the prestigious *Sunday Times* had been left out. The paper sent down a London lawyer who promptly threatened to apply for the court to be moved to the Town Hall if its reporter could not get in. The number of press seats was increased to 37. Each reporter was issued with a blue ticket for the duration, and the representatives of the public (now reduced to 16) had yellow passes handed out daily.

Participants began to arrive shortly after 10 a.m. Clement Freud's well-known face was a surprise

15

amongst the earliest: the Liberal MP is a close friend of Thorpe's and spent the first day in court beside him.

Then came faces new to the public and most of the press. David Holmes, a Manchester merchant banker and another of Thorpe's close friends; and two Welsh businessmen – George Deakin and John Le Mesurier, both of whom had met Thorpe already in Minehead, on that August day when all four had been charged. They drove up one by one among the arriving lawyers. Across the road the crowd of about a hundred tugged at each others' sleeves as a gleaming brown Rolls-Royce swung through the gates. It was driven by Sir David Napley, Thorpe's solicitor, who was insisting on the old-fashioned full hearing.

Inside the court were mounds of books and exhibits. Bilious yellow ring-bind folders entitled 'Alleged Conspiracy to Kill Norman Scott' were heaped up on the lawyers' table amongst statements and papers. The scarlet dust jackets of a book, *The Pencourt File*, added splashes of colour. The small size of the court room – 30 by 36 feet – made for an intimate atmosphere. But the three large windows on either side, high ceilings, and light oak panelling combined to give a manageable sense of space. New strip lighting had been installed which would burn throughout the day. In deference to the importance of the case, a new Royal Court of Arms had been bolted up above the magistrates' heads. As everybody sat expectantly, the court clerk, Frederick Winder, peered down from the Bench into the well of the court to check that the lawyers were ready. The four defendants and the police were down there too: the raised dock had been allotted to the press. Satisfied, the clerk opened the large wooden double doors behind the three green leather-bound chairs. The hubbub died down as he ushered the magistrates in, at 10.27 a.m. They bowed to the court and sat. The four defendants were shepherded into a line, Holmes appreciably taller than the other three.

The clerk read the charges to each of them individually. They were addressed in alphabetical order: George Deakin, 38, gaming machine distributor and club owner, of Port Talbot, West Glamorgan; David Malcolm Holmes, 48, merchant banker, of Eaton Place, London; John Le Mesurier, 46, businessman, of St Brides Major, South Glamorgan; John Jeremy Thorpe, 49, Member of Parliament, of Orme Close, Bayswater, London. All were charged: 'that on divers days between October 1 1968 and November 1 1977, in the county of Devon and elsewhere, you conspired together and with others to murder Norman Scott'. For Thorpe alone there was a second charge: between 1 January 1969 and 30 March 1969 he unlawfully incited Holmes to murder Scott.

As this was no trial, but a committal, the defendants were not required to plead 'Guilty' or 'Not Guilty'. They stayed silent. Winder came to another routine formality. The four could apply for the restrictions on press reporting, which would otherwise stay in place, to be lifted. As the reporters exchanged gloomy glances, Gareth Williams QC suddenly got to his feet. 'I wish to apply for restrictions to be lifted. My client, George Deakin, welcomes the fullest scrutiny,' he said.

All attention switched to the three magistrates. In the middle was the solid figure of the chairman, Edward Donati, a local architect retired from practice; on his left sat James Henderson, grey-haired and bespectacled, who drove an Alfa Romeo sports car but was now less active on his farm; to Donati's right was the plump figure of Mrs Margaret Griffiths, well-known in the area for her voluntary work. Her Triumph Herald was carefully parked outside.

Winder, in his capacity as the magistrates' legal adviser, whispered up to them: 'There's no discretion.' The Act lays down that if one defendant applies for restrictions to be lifted, the magistrates have no choice but to lift them for everybody involved. Donati complied, and the senior of the two Crown counsel, Peter Taylor QC, rose to his feet.

The press benches erupted in a mixture of excitement and panic. Evening paper reporters rushed for the door to phone their editors. For once the old press cliché, 'Clear the Front Page,' was true. In London reporters with good shorthand were pulled from their desks and told: 'Get down to Minehead – now.' The only railway marked on the map was run by a local steam preservation society and petered out a few miles up the coast. 'Get a taxi then!' one reporter was told. The bill was £60.

Back in court there was a hush as Taylor began. 'In 1959 Jeremy Thorpe became an MP,' he said. 'In the early 1960s he had a homosexual relationship with Norman Scott.' The first sentences were as bald as the rest of Taylor's ninety-minute opening speech. With no jury to impress he did not go for rhetoric. The bluntness echoed his northern origins – the son of a doctor, he had gone from Newcastle Grammar to Cambridge and had chosen the law. At the age of 48 he was now leader of the North East Circuit and a Crown Court recorder. Taylor – as he was later to remind the court – had already had previous experience of marathon conspiracy trials in the cases surrounding the jailed Pontefract architect, John Poulson.

As he spoke the four defendants had decided on their own places and scattered themselves around the court. Thorpe sat conspicuously alone, on the front bench below the press, in a dark grey three-piece suit with his habitual gold watch chain across the waistcoat. He looked almost as if he was listening to a speech on the green leather front bench of the House of Commons. But his face was grim. From behind, the press men saw only the back of his head and his distinctive jaw line with its perpetual five o'clock shadow. Two plain bevelled gold rings and the signet ring, all on the little finger of his left hand, contrasted with the heavy black hairs on his wrist as he pulled his pen from his inside pocket.

Across the court sat Thorpe's black-haired second wife, Marion. Her face an expressionless mask as it would be for much of the weeks that followed, she had driven into court with him and would be there to support her husband every single day. Usually she wore a bottle-green coat draped over her shoulders, and once a powder-grey tweed cloak. It was a strange occasion for a former member of the Royal Family: Marion, like her husband, had been married before – to the Earl of Harewood, King George V's grandson. They had met when Marion was a young concert pianist and were divorced in 1967 after eighteen years. Lord Harewood, with the Queen's consent, remarried. It was six years later, at Paddington Register Office, that she had married the Leader of the Liberal Party. Beside her in the public benches, day after day, sat Thorpe's mother, Mrs Ursula Thorpe. Tall and erect, with immaculately-styled upswept grey hair and, occasionally, a pair of dark glasses, she only disappeared from her place in court when her son's alleged male lover gave his testimony.

Taylor was forging on emotionlessly. 'Scott was a danger to his reputation and his career, a danger of which Mr Thorpe was constantly reminded. Scott was pestering him for help and telling others about it. Mr Thorpe's anxiety became obsessive.' The case itself began in 1961, he said, when Jeremy Thorpe was a 32-year-old bachelor MP. Norman Scott, 21 and unmarried, was interested in training horses. He went to the House of Commons in London to see Thorpe for help after a nervous breakdown. 'Jeremy Thorpe took him that very night to his mother's home in Oxted.' Their homosexual relationship was to last, on and off, until 1963. In the first of many references in the days that stretched ahead, Taylor introduced the 'Broomhills Hotel lunch': 'Thorpe and Scott stayed in the hotel afterwards, and again sex relationships took place.'

The defence lawyers were strung out along the bench beside Taylor, listening carefully and taking the occasional note. The scene did not look like the traditional British court-room: none of the barristers wore wigs and robes in this lower court and among them was an unusual figure, Sir David Napley, who was not a barrister at all but a solicitor. Solicitors have the 'right of audience' in magistrates' courts, and Sir David had intrigued the legal profession by deciding to handle Thorpe's case at committal himself. A small man with a bald head that glistened under the strip lighting and a series of elegant suits, he was a most distinguished lawyer, past President of the Law Society and author of a widely used text-book, *The Technique of Persuasion*, in which it is explained how fledgling lawyers can make best use of full-scale committal proceedings. He is also a former Conservative parliamentary candidate and chairman of Mario and Franco Restaurants Ltd.

To his right sat the other defence barristers. Gareth Williams QC, George Deakin's defence counsel, had been called to the Bar in 1965 and was working out of Pump Court in the Temple. He came from Swansea and practised on the Wales and Chester circuit. Of all the barristers he was the most aggressive with the witnesses.

Next to him was John Scannell, counsel for John Le Mesurier. At the end of the row, on the far right, sat John Mathew, David Holmes's QC. Son of Sir Theobald Mathew, he was highly experienced: before he 'took silk' in 1977, he was first senior Crown prosecuting counsel for three years. He plays backgammon and, like Sir David, belongs to the Garrick Club.

Taylor was now describing a Swiss trip made by Scott in early 1963, followed by his departure to Ireland. 'At this point he had two major problems. First he had handed over his National Insurance card to Mr Thorpe. He never got it back despite frequent requests. Secondly, he lacked his luggage which had been left in Switzerland. It contained a number of compromising letters written by Thorpe to Scott.' In 1965 Scott sat down and wrote the 'Dublin letter' which, the Crown was to maintain, later played a key part in events. Scott wrote, not to Thorpe, but to his mother, Mrs Ursula

Thorpe, about his homosexual affair. 'As to the truth of the allegations of homosexuality, Mr Thorpe has flatly denied them in a statement to the police.'

Peter Bessell, then also a Liberal MP, found himself invited to lunch at the Ritz Hotel, and was told the story. He helped get the 'Swiss luggage' letters back, and started giving Norman Scott money and assistance. Thorpe repaid Bessell some of his expenses. In 1967, Thorpe, by then Leader of the Party, confided in another friend. He chose David Holmes, best man at his first wedding. [Thorpe married Caroline Allpass in 1968. She died in a car accident two years later.] Holmes was also a prominent member of the Liberal Party and at one stage its deputy treasurer.

While Taylor spoke, Holmes, the second defendant, had found what was to be his customary position on the bench below the dock, across the room from Thorpe. Lanky and reserved, he sat wearing his huge square fashion spectacles, with only a faint smile from time to time as parts of the evidence unfolded.

By the end of 1967, the Leader of the Liberal Party was depressed, Taylor said. The problem of Norman Scott would not go away. He wanted David Holmes to kill him, and the Leader's room in the House of Commons at Westminster was the scene of detailed talk of murder between the three Liberals.

Taylor permitted himself a rare break in the narrative flow here. He described Thorpe's ensuing remark as 'ironic'. Thorpe had said: ' "It's no worse than shooting a sick dog." ' With that phrase Taylor wrote the headlines which were to blaze across the world's news the next day. Thorpe stretched out his left hand along the back of his bench: there was not a cough or murmur in court. No one shifted position for fear of missing another word.

Events came to the temporary rescue of Norman Scott when he got married. But Thorpe still favoured the 'ultimate solution'. Bessell and Holmes went through the 'American charade' of pretending they had tried and failed to get Scott to America to kill him. Soon divorced, Norman Scott met a widow, Gwen Parry-Jones, and the pair of them went to the Liberal Party with Scott's story in 1971.

Taylor now shifted the locale of his story to Devon, two years later. Scott was depressed once more and had been talking to a freelance reporter called Gordon Winter. The February 1974 General Election was in prospect. Scott's own doctor gave Scott £2500, which had come from Holmes, in exchange for more letters: 'He [the doctor] took them to Holmes, who burnt them,'

Holmes got his money back, Taylor asserted. Thorpe persuaded a generous businessman from the Bahamas to give £10,000, supposedly for election expenses. It was channelled via Jersey straight to Holmes.

But Scott remained a threat throughout 1974. The *Sunday Mirror* got hold of the 'Dublin letter' to Thorpe's mother and other documents from workmen cleaning out an old office of Bessell's. The newspaper handed the originals back to Thorpe himself but kept photocopies. 'Thorpe knew damaging material was in the offing.'

Some time that year Holmes agreed Scott would definitely have to be killed. In his work as a finance and tax consultant, Holmes knew a man called John Le Mesurier with a discount carpet business in South Wales.

In the court-room Le Mesurier, bulky and bespectacled, did not show a great deal of interest when his name was mentioned. High politics or homosexuality had nothing directly to do with him, and he spent long periods during the hearing doing newspaper crosswords, or reading weekly gardening magazines; sometimes he put up his feet on the bench in front of him. His car sported a Swansea rugby club sticker on the back.

Taylor was now putting together more pieces of the prosecution jigsaw. Le Mesurier had introduced

Bessell got an unusual invitation to lunch at the Ritz Hotel from his old friend and fellow West Country MP, Jeremy Thorpe, in the spring of 1965, Winder repeated into the machine. The House of Commons or the Reform Club would have been more normal spots, but Thorpe wanted privacy. Thorpe had already confided, in the Commons Members' dining-room, that he was a homosexual. But then he handed over a letter Thorpe's mother had received. Bessell was now given the original 'Dublin letter', hand-written on aquamarine paper, to study as it was read out in court.

'"Dear Mrs Thorpe, for the last five years, as you probably know, Jeremy and I have had a homosexual relationship. . . ."' When the writer first visited Thorpe's mother's home at Oxted, Thorpe had introduced him as a cameraman. '"Through meeting Jeremy that day, I gave birth to this vice that lies latent in every man."' Thorpe took him to lunch with people called the Colliers. '"He didn't come to me as a friend but only as a . . . oh, I hate to write that, but it upset me terribly. I was rather sick because, you see, I was looking for a friend in the real sense of the word."' The writer had been taken back to Thorpe's flat one night. '"When he had satisfied himself, he put me to sleep on a hard, lumpy, camp bed. I realized he didn't care for me. Then I decided life could not go on in this way. I told a doctor the story minus the names."' There was a spell in a clinic, becoming addicted to drugs: '"Homosexually, as I was being kept under sedation, I was cured, but of course when I left there I went straight back to Jeremy."' A horse had fallen on him in Ireland, fracturing his vertebrae. '"Bills started coming in."'

'"Your son offered me £2 after he had satisfied himself. He really is a very splendid person."' There had been a suicide attempt. '"They asked me why I had done it. Could I tell them? – No: I am too loyal, the quality your son fails at miserably."' Eventually he had got a job in Switzerland and went there penniless, to find a loft with no light or water. It smelt of horse manure. He could not get his luggage. Here he was now – in Eire, with no wages. '"A priest advised me to ask Jeremy to lend me the money to at least get my luggage back. You see, I have no clothes and life is impossible. I got somebody to ring Jeremy, who was very sweet and said: 'I have spent £30 on Norman and his luggage and phone calls.'

'"This was the last straw. Was our love to be measured in monetary value? £30 is so little, I was hurt."' He went on: '"Jeremy could lend me the money, but won't ... it is so easy to say 'Norman must start for himself' ... will you ask Jeremy to please lend me the money for at least the luggage?"' There was a change of mood in the letter: '"Jeremy owes me nothing, possibly I owe him something. ... I promise I shall repay every penny. ... I am in desperate straits or I shouldn't be asking."' A postscript said the woman he was to have married had found out about Jeremy and his 'cast-off friend' – '"hence I shall probably remain single ... please believe me, I am so desperate for help."' It was signed '"Norman Josiffe."'

Bessell said: 'I asked Thorpe if it was basically correct. He said it was.' Bessell told his friend he would go to Dublin and try to assess the situation. 'I think it relieved him greatly. He proceeded to eat his lunch, I would say almost ravenously.' Scott was duly seen, warned about blackmail and told if he persisted he could find himself in serious trouble: 'He might well be charged with a criminal offence and an application made for his extradition from Ireland.' Bessell also gave him £5, heard again his complaints about his missing luggage, and talked to the priest, Father Sweetman.

Thorpe was worried too, about police enquiries in Devon and London: 'He was anxious that this might result in a disclosure of his relationship.' Through George Thomas, then Minister of State at the Home Office, Bessell arranged a meeting with the Home Secretary, Sir Frank Soskice. Sir Frank had been '"sympathetic"', Bessell told Thorpe, but had referred to a number of letters. 'Thorpe said there had been corre-spondence between him and Scott.'

Scott's luggage returned to him in an unusual way. What Bessell understood from his own private secret-ary and from Thorpe himself was this: they had col-lected the luggage from the railway terminal them-selves, and it was taken to Thorpe's own flat at Mar-sham Court. 'Thorpe had opened it and removed a bundle of letters written by him, to Mr Scott.' Then they had sent it on to Dublin.

(Later, in a written statement, Mrs Diana Attabey was to testify that she had been Bessell's private secre-tary at the two-roomed office of 'Peter Bessell Incor-porated'. She collected a large suitcase for him from Victoria Station and took it to the offices in Clarges Street. The same evening, Thorpe rang her at her Islington flat – something he had never done before. '"Diana darling, are you in a gorgeous negligée?"' the call started. Mrs Attabey said Thorpe seemed 'pleased and relaxed' that the luggage was at Clarges Street. 'I was not present when the luggage was opened.')

In 1967, Jeremy Thorpe became the leader of Bes-sell's Party. His 'personal problems' must not be pub-licly disclosed, Bessell advised: 'Thorpe's response was, if anything of that sort became public, he would take his life.' Taylor asked him artlessly: 'Take whose life?' 'His own life,' Bessell replied.

It was 1 p.m. The court broke up excitedly for lunch, the reporters shaken out of their usual cynicism. They hastily checked some of the more extraordinary phrases with each other as they ran out of the court and up the road, towards any telephone they could find or hire. Thorpe, grim-faced during the morning, at least had one big smile as he drove away for lunch. The pupils of the school across the road had gathered along the rail-ings in their grey cardigans to cheer, and he gave them a delighted wave back.

In the afternoon Bessell described letters from Scott which culminated in an invitation to the Commons, to see what could be done. Bessell told him he would make representations to the Health ministry to get him a new Insurance card and that he would pay him a small retainer, £5 a week, in return for Scott leaving the matter in his hands. Bessell saw Thorpe, and told him what he had done. 'He said he would reimburse me for the costs involved.' Over twenty letters were produced in court which had been sent with the retainers over about eighteen months. Scott had also been given £75 to set him up in a modelling career. 'I estimate the total would have been between £600 and £700,' said Bessell. 'Mr Thorpe reimbursed about £400.'

In the spring of 1968 Scott disclosed he still had two letters from Thorpe. When Bessell passed the news on, Thorpe was 'alarmed': he suggested David Holmes should pose as a reporter, offering to buy Scott's story and getting the letters from him on the pretext they were the proof he needed to show to the editor. Thorpe, Bessell and Holmes discussed the plan in the House of Commons and Holmes agreed, but it was aborted when Scott came to Bessell's office in Pall Mall and said the letters had been destroyed.

The subject of Scott came up again more seriously just before Christmas that year when Bessell and Thorpe were in the leader's room at the House of Commons, waiting for a Division bell. 'Thorpe was depressed.... I felt it was a situation that was extremely troublesome but could be contained.' Thorpe was now married and Scott was leading a moderately successful modelling career.

'Mr Thorpe referred to it as being "a black cloud hanging over him" and was not consoled. He said he thought eventually it would be publicly exposed and that it would ruin his career.' At this point the Division bell had rung. After the Commons vote, Thorpe again raised the question of whether Scott could not be found employment in America. Bessell said it was impossible, because he could not get a work permit.

'Thorpe said: "Then we have to get rid of him." My

reaction was not one of great surprise, but at the same time I did not take it very seriously, and I decided to treat it lightly. I said: "Are you suggesting killing him off?" Thorpe stood up and looked at me, and said: "Yes." At that stage, I believed Thorpe was at that moment serious.'

Thorpe poured himself a drink and returned to his desk. Bessell, humouring 'Thorpe's mood of the moment', pointed to the practical difficulties – like disposing of the body. 'Mr Thorpe replied it could be buried somewhere. He suggested he had read somewhere of a body being placed under the rubble of a motorway, and the cement machines covering it over the next day. I answered that if he had read about it, it proved the body had been found.' The tense atmosphere in the court evaporated slightly, and there was a ripple of laughter.

Thorpe then suggested weighting the body and dropping it into a river. Bessell pointed out there were few deep rivers in Britain not surrounded by buildings. 'I really wanted to bring the discussion to a close, because I thought it was both unhealthy and really rather ridiculous, and I changed the subject.' He started talking about his Bodmin constituency. 'I must have mentioned tin mines. Mr Thorpe jumped up. I got up from my seat. He grabbed my shoulders and said: "That's it! The body can be disposed of by dropping it down a mine shaft." I recalled some time before I had told him of a mine shaft in the grounds of the home of a mutual friend, and how that friend had illustrated the depth by throwing pebbles down it, and there was a long delay between throwing the pebble, and the faint plop as it reached the water-logged workings below.

'I protested that it was morally wrong to discuss murdering someone. His phrase was: "It is no worse than shooting a sick dog." He said if Scott's story became known and was accepted, he would feel obliged to take his own life because of the damage it would cause to the Liberal Party.' Bessell left Thorpe, saying: '"You must work it out for yourself,"' but returned a few minutes later, and found Thorpe sitting with his head down. 'He said he had been thinking, and the person to kill Mr Scott would be Mr Holmes.'

Holmes, sitting opposite the witness box, showed no reaction.

Bessell went on: 'I said it was ridiculous. Holmes was too wet – I am sorry to say this, I did not regard Holmes as being competent to do it. He said neither he or I could do it. (I agreed with that.) Holmes was totally loyal and if he was properly instructed he would carry out the task.'

Taylor looked up at him: 'At no stage were you prepared to participate in any plan?' Bessell looked straight at the magistrates, who had sat silent as this story unrolled. 'Certainly not,' he said firmly.

Holmes was invited down to London in January 1969, a few weeks later, specially to discuss the plan. Bessell arrived at Thorpe's room at the House – Holmes was already there – and Thorpe had the door bolted. They were busy discussing the original 'reporter' plan, in which Holmes would pose as a representative of the German magazine, *Der Spiegel*. He was to drive Scott to Plymouth, on the pretext that the editor happened to be there. When they arrived there was to be a message left, saying the editor had moved on to Cornwall and they were to follow. 'Holmes was to take Scott to a public house, get him drunk, drive him on to the Cornish moors and shoot him. This was described as a serious plan. Holmes was sitting on the edge of the sofa with a look of disbelief on his face. Obviously, he was as astonished by the suggestion as I had been originally. I had an opportunity to wink at him, and he relaxed.'

Bessell, adjusting his black-rimmed half-moon glasses, peered over them, and described how he had again raised practical objections. There would be the noise of the gun and Scott was a large man. Dragging his body to a mine shaft would obviously leave a trail of blood. 'Mr Thorpe said: "In that case it will have to be poison." He said it would be quite simple to drop poison into Mr Scott's drink at a public house.'

Holmes had 'a considerable sense of humour', Bessell added. 'He said it would look rather odd, if Scott dropped dead off the bar stool. I too have a sense of humour. I said he could apologize to the landlord and ask the directions to the nearest mine shaft.'

Did Thorpe have a sense of humour? asked Taylor. Bessell made one of his lengthy pauses. 'Mr Thorpe has a wonderful sense of humour,' he said acidly. 'Mr Thorpe and I had a sense of humour which bordered on the ridiculous; we could laugh at things other people did not find funny. But on this occasion Mr Thorpe did not respond, and chided me for not taking the matter seriously. He said it was a simple matter of research for a suitable poison. He was not prepared to be put off by the objections we were raising.' Thorpe said they could use a slow-acting poison instead of an instantly-acting one. It was left to Bessell and Holmes to investigate, and the meeting broke up.

Holmes and Bessell went to the Strangers' cafeteria in the Commons, to discuss the proposal. 'Mr Holmes had not been entirely surprised by it, but he had been surprised Mr Thorpe had suggested him for the role of the murderer. He knew, as I knew, Mr Thorpe was obsessed by the problem of Scott.' They agreed to keep in touch privately with the object of delaying reporting back as long as possible, in the hope Thorpe would quickly forget about the scheme.

A few months later, Thorpe re-convened the meeting for a progress report. But Bessell had some news for him. Scott had got married on 13 May 1969. 'Mr Thorpe seemed relieved by the marriage. He accepted it removed the plan that had been evolved as impractical, but said we knew nothing of Scott's wife and it would have been better if the "ultimate solution" could have been used.' The plan would be shelved for the time being. 'Holmes's reaction was one of relief.'

But the Scott problem had not gone away. In August he rang Bessell in a 'hysterical state' saying that because of his lack of Insurance card, he could not get maternity benefits for his wife. Later, in 1970, there was worse news. Scott's marriage had broken up. 'Mr Thorpe viewed the possibility of divorce proceedings in court with alarm. We were both sure Scott would make it an opportunity to state in court, his trouble stemmed from his relationship with Thorpe.'

The two MPs decided to appoint Leonard Ross, a solicitor they had both used, to act for Scott in the divorce proceedings, 'with the view to persuading Scott to keep Thorpe's name out of the matter'. Thorpe had agreed, but came back to the idea of killing Scott. 'Thorpe said it would be the only solution which could finally resolve the problem.'

Bessell, who had refused an earlier offer to sit down, was obviously flagging by now. Speaking ever more slowly, he described how he and Holmes were both going to America in January 1971. 'Thorpe suggested it would be an opportunity, as we were both going to be in the States together, if Scott obtained a visa, for Holmes to kill Scott.'

The court broke up for the day at 4.30 p.m., and the Somerset dusk was wiped out by the white blaze of TV lamps and flash bulbs as Thorpe's Rover nosed down the driveway, through the crowds, and across Exmoor to his Cobbaton home. Marion was beside him.

The next morning at ten, Donati, the chairman of the magistrates, performed his duty. 'I have to remind you that reporting restrictions have been lifted in these proceedings.' No one needed a reminder. The papers had gone to town. 'Murder Plot at the House', 'Like Shooting Sick Dog', ran the headlines. The tabloid *Sun* had thrown away its Page Three pin-up for a picture of Scott (fully clothed) sitting in a chintz armchair. The *Daily Mail*, with seven full pages on the hearing, was already labelling it 'The Case of The Century'.

Thorpe walked right up to the foot of the press

benches, and stood staring deliberately at the journalists jammed shoulder to shoulder for another day of sensations. There was a muttered chorus of 'Good morning.' Thorpe, apparently satisfied with this response, settled himself down in front of them. Everyone waited for Bessell to resume.

'Mr Thorpe tended to be discouraged when he found the thing was impossible, and to move on to more fruitful activities,' Bessell announced. Therefore, he and Holmes decided to mount 'the American charade'. Bessell was due to be in Miami: Holmes met him there in a rented car, with a toy gun in the back by way of a joke: '"I'll be able to say to Thorpe I was able to obtain a gun!"' he said. The idea, which was Thorpe's, was to kill Scott somewhere in the remote Florida interior. Holmes was supposed to do the shooting, and there were progress reports reassuring Thorpe all was ready: 'Of course, we knew Scott was safe in North Wales and was not coming to Miami . . . we would build up Mr Thorpe's hopes and then at the end, when we were able to show it was impractical, we would let him down suddenly. It would be the best way of persuading him that every effort had been made, and the scheme was totally impossible.'

It seemed to work. Holmes rang Bessell up later, reporting Thorpe was preoccupied with the efforts of the lawyer, Ross, to persuade Scott not to defend his divorce. 'He reported that . . . as far as the murder plan was concerned, he regarded Holmes and I as incompetent idiots, but since there was no one else able to carry out the plan, Holmes was confident we'd heard the last of it.'

Taylor now steered Bessell towards the Liberal Party's own investigations of the Scott allegations in 1971. Bessell, who reeled off eight hours in all of events and detailed conversations, momentarily 'died'. 'Did you speak to anybody else in the Liberal Party?' There was silence – 'I have a blank of memory' – 'Yes, yes, now I know . . . the reason I didn't place it, was this was several months later, in May or June 1971.' The Liberal MP Emlyn Hooson phoned him: the call sent Bessell round to Thorpe's flat at Ashley Gardens: 'I told him of the conversation I had had with Mr Hooson . . . it was that Scott had been in touch with Hooson. . . . Hooson's attitude was that Mr Thorpe would be compelled to resign the leadership of the Liberal Party.' Thorpe's response was to ring up David Steel MP, and then Hooson himself: he tape-recorded what he said to them.

Bessell was mostly in America during the next three years and heard little more about Scott, although, on a plane between New York and Washington in early 1973, Thorpe said he wanted them to meet in London, as the Scott matter had still not been cleared up. Bessell's American and English businesses failed in January 1974. After four days in Mexico, he settled down in California, where he had stayed ever since.

At Christmas 1975 came the 'Holmes mission'. Holmes told Bessell on the phone that Thorpe was 'worried'. Holmes then turned up in California with his male travelling companion, Gerald Hagan. Over dinner at Bessell's Oceanside cottage, Holmes told him a 'rather theatrical, but not at all impossible' story. A disaster faced Mr Thorpe's career, because of a pending court case.

Scott, it seemed, 'had struck up an acquaintance with an airline pilot. He was a married man, but promiscuous, and Scott had managed to get hold of photographs of the airline pilot with a girl – I think both of them in the nude. He had been blackmailing the pilot with threats of showing the photographs to his wife.

'I expressed surprise because I said that, in my dealings with Scott, whatever his faults might be, he was not in my experience a blackmailer.' Holmes told him: '"Scott has greatly deteriorated in recent years."' Scott and the pilot had been quarrelling on Exmoor when the pilot produced a gun and shot dead Scott's dog, he continued. The pilot told a passing police patrol he had shot the dog in self-defence, but would shoot Scott himself next time: 'He was sick of being blackmailed.'

Bessell, rather facetiously, asked what breed of dog was involved. 'This seemed to irritate Holmes, and he said I didn't seem to be taking the matter seriously enough.' Scott had been going round north Devon spreading his usual rumours to reporters, and trying to publish a book. He was bound to use a privileged court platform to talk about Thorpe. Bessell, unimpressed, thought Thorpe must be 'over-reacting' as usual. He assured him any Scott outburst 'would appear to be the ravings of a layabout, who had turned to blackmail for a living'.

The court took a break. Thorpe strolled over to the public benches, where Marion fed him Polo mints. A young barrister, sent down by the Liberal Party to report on the proceedings for the present Liberal Leader, David Steel, stayed in his seat just behind the former party leader. Thorpe chatted to him from time to time.

What changed Bessell's mind, he said when he resumed, was Holmes's introduction of the prominent lawyer, Lord Goodman, into the conversation. Holmes assured him it was Goodman's opinion that a Scott outburst could have grave consequences. 'When I heard Lord Goodman was taking it seriously, and knowing his reputation as a fine lawyer . . . I said: "What can I do?"' Holmes proposed the Barnes letter. 'Holmes said Lord Goodman had suggested I should write a letter to Scott's solicitors, saying Scott had blackmailed me, years before,' Bessell said. Goodman would then warn that if Thorpe's name was mentioned in court, Scott himself would face jail for blackmail. 'I was startled . . . Scott had never blackmailed me. If Scott or his solicitor called my bluff, I would have to say there was no truth in the story, since the only matter about which Scott could have blackmailed me would have been over his relationship with Thorpe.'

That had been thought of, Holmes told him. Thorpe

and Goodman wanted Bessell to say the blackmail was over either his personal business affairs or a relationship with a woman. But Scott knew nothing of his business or love affairs, said Bessell. He did not want to put himself at risk, having lost his business, made a settlement with his creditors and set about rehabilitating himself. The father of Diane Kelly (the woman he was living with) had spent a lot of money to give him a new chance in life.

Bessell would never be called upon to give evidence, Holmes assured him. If Bessell wrote a letter, it would never even become public. He handed over a present from Jeremy Thorpe. It was a book – *Life with Lloyd George*, by A. J. Sylvester. The inscription in it ran: '"For Peter from Jeremy with affection. From one Liberal to another Liberal about a third Liberal. 'Vive Les Trois Mousquetiers.' New Year, 1976."' The Three Musketeers could hardly be Lloyd George, Thorpe and Bessell, Bessell reasoned: it must be Thorpe, Bessell and Holmes. 'Holmes drew my attention to chapter nine, I think, that deals with Lloyd George's fears that his relationship with Frances Stevenson, Lloyd George's secretary, might become public.'

Now Holmes followed up with a letter from Thorpe. It had been written ambiguously in case Holmes met with an accident, he warned. Before Jeremy starts confusing things, Bessell said, couldn't he just say Scott was *attempting* blackmail? He was about to open the letter at last. '"Wait a moment! There's another matter I haven't told you about,"' said Holmes. Scott had kept many of the letters Bessell had sent while he was trying to help him with his Insurance card and a passport. Thorpe regarded them as dangerous confirmation of Scott's story and they had been bought from Scott for £10,000. '"Where on earth did you get the money?"' Holmes hesitated for a moment and then said it was his money. I was surprised. Holmes was comfortably off, but not the kind of person who would have £10,000 in cash to spend on a matter of this sort.'

Bessell changed his mind; he would now do what Thorpe wanted. 'Scott, £10,000 better off, was 10,000 times more dangerous:' he would have an inflated idea of himself, and the danger he represented to Thorpe. Bessell at last opened the letter. Thorpe asked his friend to say that £10,000 had been found for Bessell himself by Diane Kelly's father, Mr Fred Miller. 'I rejected that out of hand.' Thorpe went on to reassure him: '"The press will never be able to find you."' Holmes was 'slightly confused' about whether this letter of Bessell's was to go to Scott's solicitor or the pilot's solicitor. The address he gave him in Devon was of a Mr Michael Barnes. Thorpe had also sent a draft letter for Bessell to write. It started, '"I feel I owe you an explanation regarding Mr Norman Scott."'

'I didn't see I owed anybody an explanation . . . it also made reference to the £10,000 being provided by my present father-in-law.'

Bessell finally typed his own letter to Barnes. Scott was a 'mentally sick' and 'vicious' person, who he had been helping, as an MP, with his National Insurance problems, and to whom he had given office work out of charity. Scott had threatened to expose an affair he was having with his secretary unless Bessell gave him money. Bessell had done so.

With this missive, Bessell sent a personal note to Thorpe remarking how young David Holmes was still looking. Having apparently flushed the letter from Thorpe down the toilet, Holmes rang up 'Marion' in London and left a message for Thorpe. '"Mission Accomplished,"' it read. 'I was really disgusted with myself for the letter I had just written and didn't wish to speak to Thorpe just then. . . . It was a disgraceful letter,' Bessell continued.

But the phrase 'Mission Accomplished' bothered him. Driving Holmes back to the airport with the newly written 'Barnes letter', he demanded to know what was going on. 'Holmes hesitated, and then said: "Very well, the airline pilot was hired to shoot Scott." I said: "Oh

39

Christ, David! I thought all ideas of that sort had been abandoned a long time ago. . . . Who hired the pilot?'' Holmes said: ''I did.''

'I replied: ''I'm appalled. You and I have always worked together to ensure nothing of that sort could happen.'' Holmes said: ''Everything has changed.''' Scott had done nothing but make trouble since he moved to north Devon. He was a far greater threat than ever, and there was no alternative but to dispose of him. 'I said: ''Thank God, it failed.'' Holmes, agreeing, said: ''Yes. And it never can be tried again.'' It was obvious he was sincere.' He mumbled something about having found the airline pilot through friends, and that he was offered £5000. Bessell now wanted the letter back, but it took him so long to park the car at the airport that Holmes's and Hagan's plane had left with them and the letter aboard by the time Bessell got back to the terminal.

In the New Year (1976), Bessell heard the cat was out of the bag. Holmes rang him on 1 February. At a minor court appearance, 'Scott had made the outburst which Holmes and Thorpe feared and expected would be made at the trial of the airline pilot.' On Lord Goodman's advice, Thorpe had issued a very brief denial. 'I can remember his [Holmes's] precise words. They were: ''Lord Goodman has advised that if you are accused of stealing an apple, it's better to say: 'I didn't steal it,' than to say: 'I never eat apples, and I was in New York at the time,' since the more you say, the more opportunity there is for questions.'''

Now Thorpe himself rang Bessell up twice. Extracts from the Barnes letter had been leaked to the press. Bessell was appalled: 'It would destroy the remnants of my already shattered reputation. I was desperately sorry about what had happened . . . but clearly I had to issue a denial.' Thorpe told him Cyril Smith, the Liberal Chief Whip, having seen the letter in confidence, had leaked it. 'Without Thorpe's consent, Cyril Smith had disseminated its contents to the press,' Bessell said. Thorpe had added: '''Peter, I am begging for time. Let

40

me get this thing under control and we can issue a joint statement."'

Bessell slowly described the rest of the conversation in his extravagantly rich, brown voice. He informed Thorpe he had already denied to the *Daily Mail* that he had sworn an affidavit saying the letter was true. 'Thorpe said: "Well, I'll have to sue someone sooner or later. It might as well be the *Daily Mail*." I reminded him of the Oscar Wilde case. "If you sue someone for libel, far too much will come out." He said: "I know, I know." He sounded very depressed.'

Why not stick to the cover story that Bessell's retainer payments were a mere act of charity to a con-stituent with National Insurance problems? '"Use-less,"' said Thorpe. Why didn't Bessell say instead that, as he might have to give evidence, he was obliged to say: 'No comment'?

'I almost lost my mind! I was stunned . . . I had always been assured there was no question of my being asked to give evidence . . . this whole thing had become public and completely disrupted my life and indeed, for a short time, my thinking processes. I asked Thorpe: "Is it true that David Holmes paid £10,000 for my letters to Scott?"' Thorpe replied instantly: '"Not to my knowledge."' Bessell said: '"Then in that case the whole thing is a cock-and-bull story . . . the letter was going to be used as a cover for Scott's outburst."' Thorpe said: '"Wait. Let me give you an Isaac Foot answer."' (Bessell explained: both he and Thorpe had known the former Bodmin MP well. 'It meant he was speaking to me privately, in a way that would not be easily understood by other people.') '"If David had taken the ferry, it was essential those letters should not be found by the police afterwards. We had to get them first."' (The original murder plan had been for Holmes to lure Scott into Cornwall. Thorpe had described how Holmes would have to take the ferry there across the Tamar, forgetting there was a new bridge – 'It almost became a joke.')

The conversation, Bessell went on, had continued like this:

'BESSELL: "I must know the truth. I want this clearly."'
'THORPE: "Is this phone line safe?"'
'BESSELL: "I don't know. I suppose it is but I must know the truth . . . so the plan David told me about was real?"'
'THORPE: "Yes."'
'BESSELL: "Well thank God it failed – that can never be tried again."'
'THORPE: "No that's right, it cannot be tried again."'
'BESSELL: "Where did Holmes get the money?"'
'THORPE [Bessell said he hesitated for a moment]: "It was David's own money."''

Taylor stopped his flow of questions for lunch.

In the afternoon Taylor asked Bessell if he was finding the day too long for his frail health, and told him if he wanted a break at any point, he could have it. Bessell nodded, and began again. George Deakin buried his head in another tabloid newspaper.

Bessell began by saying that he had asked Thorpe if he could tell his wife that the story about him being blackmailed over a woman was untrue. Thorpe seemed surprised and asked if Bessell's wife knew about the Scott affair. Bessell replied that she did, but Thorpe still refused to let him make the call. 'I asked him to telephone her, and he replied: "Yes I will. Scout's Honour."' The next day, 3 February, he had rung Thorpe. His wife, Marion, answered and Bessell was surprised she sounded so cold. When Thorpe rang back, he asked why, and Thorpe replied: '"I think that's right. All those letters. . . ." I took it from Thorpe's attitude he was passing the blame for the whole of the problem and publicity to me.'

Because Thorpe faced a meeting of the Parliamentary Liberal Party the next day, Bessell allowed the press to publish the fact he was living with Diane Kelly (his present wife) to take pressure off his friend. Thorpe said he was grateful; 'he added: "I wake up every morning with that terrible sick feeling."' The meeting of the Liberals ended with a vote of confidence in Thorpe's leadership. Bessell assumed that was the end of the matter. 'I tried to console myself with the thought that Scott was alive and unharmed, and this thing could never be attempted, or thought about, again.'

But Bessell then felt he had to withdraw the Barnes letter. He wrote to the Devon solicitor, accordingly. The reason he gave was that Cyril Smith had given a summary of the letter to the press, and he realized that, as he had had to write it hurriedly, it contained several 'serious inaccuracies'.

On 19 February 1976, a long letter came from Thorpe. It talked of four Phases. First, 'Cyril' had panicked, wrongly referred to the Barnes letter's existence, and then wrongly described its contents. A note in the margin said: '"He's opened his mouth too often!"' Phase Two was when Bessell had been '"caught on the hop"' and denied almost everything in the letter. '"I don't blame you, but it didn't enhance anybody's credibility,"' Thorpe wrote. In Phase Three Bessell had put out his statement confirming the broad outlines, and Phase Four was when '"to my horror, you now tell Barnes that you want to withdraw the letter in view of the adverse publicity"'.

Bessell should consider several things: the letter was already with the police; nobody was likely to publish it; the only result of withdrawal was to suggest the letter was a fabrication – which it was not; there might be some other explanation for the payments '"which frankly there isn't"'; and '"that we are lying like troopers, which we are not"'.

In view of the denials and counter-denials, the police might want to interview Bessell. '"My advice is a) Your letter is correct. b) You wanted to withdraw since the undertaking of confidentiality was breached. c) Scott is a Lunatic."' The fourth piece of advice was to say that he would not prefer charges of blackmail against Scott.

The letter continued:

'All the above is right if justice is to be done. The press are still being bloody and trying to destroy me. Harold, on the other hand, is being quite superb. . . . The whole story has been a nightmare but I am damned if that bloody lunatic is going to destroy me and the Party. So far I've had 700 letters in support . . . stand firm and we shall win through. You need say nothing more. Your letter is enough. Bless you. Take care of yourself and remember LL.G. [Lloyd George].

'Ever yours affectionately
'Jeremy
'Your letter was superb, to Emlyn [Hooson].
'None of us have anything to hide.'

Bessell wrote back, signing one of the letters '"Besselli"'. There was some puzzlement in court at this, and Taylor asked him to explain. Bessell permitted himself a faint smile: 'We were accustomed to all kinds of schoolboy-ish jokes between us,' he said. 'Besselli was a nickname by which Mr Thorpe usually called me.'

Bessell's response to Thorpe, in writing, was that the Barnes letter he had been asked to write '"gave the appearance of being a cover-up. Nobody seemed to believe it."' He wrote: '"Marion [Thorpe's wife] treated me like excrement on the phone and this is wholly unjustified. Can't you see it is imperative I am believed? Nixon fell because at the end he trusted no one, not even his friends. You are no Nixon, a betrayer of friends."' Pressure had perhaps been '"pummelling"' Thorpe's brain.

Taylor pointed out the letters, in summary, read as though Bessell believed Thorpe had nothing to hide. 'This is not a true reflection,' Bessell explained. They had been written like that, because they were going in the mail, and he could not be sure who would open them. 'At that stage, I had determined, as I told Mr Thorpe on the telephone, I intended to stand by him in all respects for his own sake and, as I believed, in the interests of the Liberal Party.'

But in May 1976 things had changed. 'As a result of representations made on a fairly continuous basis, by certain members of the Parliamentary Liberal Party, I agreed I would state the truth as I knew it about the relationship between Mr Thorpe and Mr Scott.' He told a reporter for the *Daily Mail* in Los Angeles that the Barnes letter was untrue and, 'I had lied for the protection of Mr Thorpe'.

The newspaper published the story. On 5 and 6 May he had telephone calls from Holmes. 'Holmes asked me to withdraw the statement given to the *Mail*, and to revert to the original story that I had been blackmailed by Scott.' Bessell refused. 'The following day, he again implored me to reverse the story. I said it was impossible. He asked me if I realized the danger I was creating for him and for Mr Thorpe. I said I did . . . I then realized he was referring to the shooting incident on Exmoor. He said we three (himself, Mr Thorpe and I) were the only ones who knew everything. He put emphasis on "everything". I said I realized that was so. But the time had come for the truth. Then he said: "There is nothing more to be said." I said: "I'm afraid not."' Bessell ended: 'I never had any further conversation with Mr Holmes after this.'

Taylor passed across two cassette tape-recordings Bessell had given to the police. He verified them gravely and slowly, before handing them back.

After eight hours in the witness box, Bessell had told a long, complicated and extraordinary story. Sir David Napley was to claim later that the whole case against Thorpe stood or fell on his evidence. And the defence lawyers were determined to make it fall.

3

Bessell cross-examined

The prosecution had expressed anxiety about Bessell's
health whilst he was giving his evidence in chief. For the
next two days of cross-examination his stamina and his
imperturbable cool was severely tested as he was subjected to a gruelling and often hostile barrage of questions centring on his character and conduct, and made a
number of admissions about himself.

The cross-examination, like his main evidence, was
also to be a severe test of both the magistrates and the
reporters crowded together on the press benches. In
any court case, the first prosecution witness's testimony
is often confusing. The lawyers cannot recall witnesses
when it suits them. They have to put all their questions
to them at once. They therefore often bring up points
whose significance only becomes apparent later, when
other witnesses fill in their pieces of the jigsaw.

In this case, the problem for the court was even
greater than usual. As Taylor had already told the
Bench, it was a very long and bizarre story and Bessell
was involved in it from the beginning – in the 1960s – to
the very end. At the same time, there was a gap in his
personal narrative. It was common ground that he had
disappeared from the story between 1973 and 1976,
and had nothing to do with the particular plan which
led, it was alleged, to the shooting of Scott's dog. But he
had played a major part in what the prosecution
claimed was a subsequent cover-up attempt.

Cross-examinations tend inevitably to dart from
point to point, as each defence lawyer asks about mat-

ters concerning his own client. Bessell did not make comprehension any easier through his insistence on meticulously phrasing every answer. As an MP for six years, he had been trained in the art of going 'on the record', and was determined none of his replies could be misinterpreted.

Neither the magistrates nor the reporters were too troubled, however, with the occasional intriguingly mysterious reference that was to emerge that day. They know most of it would make sense shortly.

Neither Williams, for Deakin, nor Scannell, for Le Mesurier, were interested in questioning Bessell, as he readily confirmed he did not know their clients. But John Mathew, for David Holmes, clearly was. Mathew was at the far end of the lawyer's bench, with his client sitting opposite Bessell. As usual during the entire proceedings, Holmes showed little emotion as he sat in his smart business suit, occasionally crossing his legs and adjusting the large spectacles which he sometimes wore, apparently at random. Like Thorpe, he sat closely listening to the proceedings, not diverting himself with newspapers like Deakin and Le Mesurier.

Mathew, enormously respected at the Bar for his vast experience of criminal cases, only occasionally looked at his witness or the magistrates when questioning. Mostly he would focus his eyes on a point on the wall straight ahead of him, only turning to stare at the person he was interrogating when pressing for an answer. He told Bessell in a withering tone that he was not concerned with the accuracy of his evidence, but only wanted to amplify parts of it. Had Holmes's reaction been the same as Bessell's when Thorpe was supposedly inciting them to arrange Scott's death – that neither were prepared to take part in any plan? Bessell replied: 'Correct.' It was also correct that he and Holmes were concerned with persuading Thorpe the plan was unworkable. 'It was a matter of gradually discouraging him over a period,' Bessell said.

That disposed of, Mathew raised the subject of Bessell's 'aide-memoire', which had been briefly mentioned earlier. Bessell said he had written this chronology of events to help his memory between September and October 1976 over a period of about three weeks. Did he have any objection to producing a full copy? Bessell said he would have to ask his solicitors, because it contained information which might cause embarrassment to others unconnected with the case. Wasn't it right that the reasons Bessell had once stated for wanting to withdraw the Barnes letter were partly untrue? Mathew grew tetchy as he pressed his point again and again. Eventually Bessell conceded the reasons were untrue.

Mathew, unlike some of the other lawyers, conducted his cross-examination by picking at small points, and making absolutely sure a precise reply was read into the depositions by Winder, the clerk. He darted from one point to another, getting Bessell to rehearse his account of what happened at the California airport after Holmes's 'Mission accomplished' telephone call, and his relationships with journalists. Had he ever appeared on television? Yes, in America on 24 September 1978. 'At a time when you had agreed to come to this country to give evidence in this case?' 'Yes.'

It was the end of the second day. Mathew said he would continue his cross-examination the following morning. But on Wednesday it was Taylor who unexpectedly rose to his feet. His subject was Lord Goodman. That morning this had appeared at the head of *The Times* letter column:

AN ALLEGATION
IN COURT
From Lord Goodman CH

Sir, May I again ask the courtesy of your happily still available columns to advise your readers that it is not possible for me to deal with the allegations made against me in the Thorpe proceedings without infringing the possibilities of a fair trial.

I hope therefore that no one will draw any conclusions from

48

my silence, it being my intention at the earliest possible
moment to make an appropriate statement.
Yours faithfully,

GOODMAN
4 Little Essex Street,
Strand, WC2.
November 21.

In fact Lord Goodman had already made further
comments. Later editions of the *Daily Telegraph*
front-paged an interview with him in which he was
quoted as saying: 'I am taking advice on whether an
innocent man is able, under our legal system, to repudi-
ate allegations made against him.

'It is apparently the case that one is unable to defend
oneself against not only baseless, but demented, allegations while proceedings are in progress.'

He proceeded to do just that. 'But who in the world
would believe that a sane man of blameless reputation,
who over the years has rendered no insignificant services to this country, could be guilty of allegations
which no small kindergarten child would believe.' He
was most concerned at the morning headlines. 'It is of
interest that the police never came near me, nor invited
me to make a statement. Nor have I had any approach
from the Director of Public Prosecutions. I heard
totally unofficially that I was to be mentioned in the
case some time back and promptly caused a leading
counsel to go round and speak to prosecuting counsel
repudiating the allegations.' In the meantime, he concluded, it would not be improper for an innocent man
to announce his innocence.

Taylor clarified the position in court with what he
described as 'A short statement on behalf of the
Crown'. He read out: 'Some of the reports in today's
newspapers, particularly the headlines, may have given
the impression there has been direct evidence of Lord
Goodman suggesting a plan in connection with Mr
Scott, and that this is part of the prosecution case. It is

not part of the prosecution case, and in effect, the evidence of Mr Bessell was not directly to that effect, but simply reporting what Mr Holmes told him (Mr Bessell) about Lord Goodman.' The first evening newspaper reporter made a hurried exit for the telephone.

Mathew continued his cross-examination. Bessell conceded he had not tape-recorded the two calls from Holmes asking him to stick by his Barnes blackmail letter. He had been at a friend's house and had not had his recording equipment. Neither had he listed them in his *aide-memoire*. When he 'recalled the incident' he had written to the police and given a statement on a supplementary form.

Mathew introduced two new names – Barrie Penrose and Roger Courtiour. The two journalists, dubbing themselves 'Pencourt', had written *The Pencourt File*. Their activities were to become a major strand running through the proceedings. The book was an unusual one, to say the least, as it charted the pair's gradual progress through the complicated affairs which led to the charging of Thorpe; the two reporters, who had originally come just to view the proceedings, were soon to realize they would face a string of allegations about their own conduct. They were later to issue a statement, printed in a letter to the *Guardian*, that at the first possible opportunity they would have answers for the various things that had been said about them, and more facts about the matter.

Bessell conceded he had had a number of long phone conversations with one or the other of the reporters, after Penrose had first rung him in May 1976. Had he tape-recorded them? Some of them, Bessell admitted, but he was not at all sure how many. Bessell's usual precision deserted him, and he had to admit that he couldn't really tell the court how many of these tapes he had. Mathew dropped this, and pressed Bessell on his telephone conversations with Holmes. Bessell eventually said he had only told police about the calls later because he thought it 'might be helpful' if he added them to his main statement. It might be that the details had been in an *addendum* to his *aide-memoire*, which would be why he hadn't told the police about them when he was interviewed in California.

Mathew finished and there was a rustle on the press benches as the reporters waited for the first attack on behalf of Thorpe. Bessell took a sip of water and stood stoically, as Sir David Napley rose. Was it true that over the years Mr Thorpe had done a number of kindnesses for him? 'Yes.' He had done numerous kindnesses for other people? 'I would not quarrel that by nature he is an exceedingly kind man.' Sir David: 'You would not quarrel with the suggestion that he is not by nature capable of any cruelty?' Bessell took several seconds to reply. Looking straight ahead, he said slowly in his deep firm voice: 'I would quarrel with that and say I think he is capable of cruelty.'

Sir David wanted to know when and why Thorpe had ceased to be his friend. It was in May 1976, when Bessell had given the interview saying he had lied to protect Thorpe. The second part of his answer was longer: 'Because I did not believe I could continue to sustain a position that was damaging to the Liberal Party, and which was a false position.'

The sweeping opening was a favourite tactic of Sir David; he was to use it later in his cross-examinations with mixed effects. He plunged into his more detailed questions. Bessell had been granted immunity by the Director of Public Prosecutions (DPP). Sir David produced a copy of the text with a flourish and read it: '"Conditional upon Mr Bessell giving evidence for the Crown at the Magistrates' Court, and if necessary in the Crown Court, in criminal proceedings against your client and others; no criminal proceedings will be instituted by the police or any other prosecuting authority against Mr Bessell in respect of matters forming part of the subject matter of the proceedings against Jeremy Thorpe and others, or in respect of matters which may be referred to in court in such proceedings, and in the event of any private prosecution of Mr Bessell in respect of any such matter, the DPP will assume responsibility for the conduct of those proceedings and offer no evidence against Mr Bessell."'

The previous week, in a hurried High Court hearing, Thorpe's lawyers had tried to have the immunity scrapped, claiming it would allow Bessell to commit perjury at Minehead. Peter Taylor had appeared for the DPP at the High Court hearing and vigorously denied this. Thorpe's lawyer had called the immunity 'an unedifying bargain' and warned that when Bessell did appear in the witness box he would be cross-examined 'about the commission of other criminal offences by him, unconnected with the subject matter of the proceedings'. The application had been turned down by the Lord Chief Justice, Lord Widgery.

Sir David now wanted to know why Bessell had taken immunity. He replied he had not asked for it at first, but had been advised to do so by his London solicitor, Mr Lionel Phillips (who was sitting in the court-room, keeping watch for Bessell). Bessell's final answer, in his wordy style, boiled down to his agreeing that he had started as a man who did not want immunity but had ended with one which Sir David described as 'wider than anything I have ever seen in the course of a long practice'.

Sir David questioned him about his health. Bessell said he was being treated for moderate to severe emphysema and the after-effects of a suspected coronary. Sir David began to dig into his background. Yes, the coronary had been at Ensenada, just across the Mexican border from the USA at the time he had 'disappeared' in January 1974.

Sir David waved a copy of *The Pencourt File*. 'Have you read it?' he asked. Bessell had. Sir David said sarcastically: 'At least you have my sympathy on that score.' Bessell agreed the phraseology in the book closely followed that of his *aide-memoire* but denied that he had given a copy of it to the journalists. They had come to see him for five to six days in California in December 1977 to get information. They had exchanged theories 'to try to arrive at the truth'. But at one point he had lied to them. 'They had a theory that there was some vast plot afoot that involved espionage and similar matters which I found it difficult to take seriously.' He denied telling them he was a secret agent: he had said he had special connections in Washington. He had done this to test their gullibility.

The next exchange showed Sir David was not going to always go unchallenged. To try to demonstrate how close Bessell was to Pencourt Sir David quoted an extract from a letter Bessell had written to Lady Falkender, Sir Harold Wilson's political secretary, in which he said: '"As you know I worked fairly closely with Barrie and Roger (the authors) in the preparation of *The Pencourt File*."' Bessell interrupted sharply, peering at a copy through his half-moon spectacles, and read the next sentence '" – although not as closely as I would have liked"'. He read further: '" – if they had confided more to me I could have steered them away from some unfortunate errors of fact and judgement"'.

Sir David shovelled his papers and brought up the next item on his list – Thorpe's alleged confession he was a homosexual, made in the spring of 1965 in the House of Commons Members' dining-room. Bessell agreed he had told Thorpe he himself had homosexual tendencies while trying to confirm his suspicions. 'A number of people had put to me at one time or another they thought he might be homosexual.' At that time he was campaigning for Thorpe as Leader of the Party.

This time it was Sir David's turn. Yes, Bessell said, he unquestionably believed Thorpe was the best person for Leader. 'And you also told Emlyn Hooson he was the best person to do it?' 'No,' said Bessell, embarking on a lengthy explanation. Sir David sharpened his questioning until Bessell conceded that he might have been telling both men the same thing at the same time.

Now came the lunch shared by Thorpe and Bessell at the Ritz. Sir David appeared astonished that Bessell could remember a conversation thirteen years previously of which he had kept no note. 'It made a great impression on me and the details are etched in my mind. It was the beginning of the acceptance by me of responsibility with regard to Mr Scott and Mr Thorpe.'

Sir David ran through the account of Bessell's meetings with Scott in Ireland, but temporarily abandoned the line of questioning when he was unable to find the relevant documents in the huge heap in front of him. The Insurance card problem was raised. Scott could not get benefits if his card was not fully stamped, and his employer was open to prosecution for failing to stamp it. 'Did you know he had been given a number and given his card as early as 1962 as a result of an intervention by Mr Thorpe?' Bessell replied: 'I had no idea of it.'

Bessell said it had been his idea to contact Sir Frank Soskice, the then Home Secretary. 'I told him the facts as I knew them.' Sir Frank (now Lord Stow Hill) had seemed to get the impression that Thorpe and Scott were anxious to see each other. Sir Frank had said: '"Tell him [Scott] to go to hell. Get rid of him."' What he had been trying to say was: '"Keep them apart."' Bessell explained: 'Get him out of Mr Thorpe's life would have been a better phrase.'

Sir Frank wrote to *The Times* saying he would make a statement in due course. (He died, at the age of 76, on 2 January 1979.)

The court adjourned. His California-cut suit hanging a little loosely on his thin frame, Bessell was driven off for lunch by his solicitor in a beige 1.3 Ford Escort.

That afternoon in court, Thorpe was in a distinctly perky mood. 'How nice to see you!' he said, enthusiastically shaking hands with a *London Evening News* man. 'How are you?' the journalist asked, and Thorpe steepled his hands in a gesture of mock prayer, much as if he had been asked what his prospects were on polling day. Marion, sitting across on the public benches, was clutching his brown trilby. Thorpe's lawyer, up at the front, worried away at Bessell, probing him aggressively on dates and places. 'Do please answer the question. . . . Do not make a speech and keep your explanation preferably short.' Bessell couldn't give precise dates. Sir David reminded him: 'The account you give of . . . ten years ago, you give in circumstantial detail, even to when someone passed out a glass of whisky.'

At last Sir David reached the major attack on Bessell and his character which he had promised the public the previous week. Bessell had disappeared from his creditors in 1974 owing no less than £350,000, he suggested.

During the ten-minute afternoon break Thorpe leaned on a bench, smiling and joking with the *Sunday Telegraph* man. Donati, the chairman of the magistrates, warned solemnly that someone had tried to bring a tape-recorder into the court. 'This is not permissible.'

Sir David dived into financial detail. It transpired Bessell owed $335,000 to his father-in-law, Fred Miller. And about £14,000 to the prominent Liberal, Lord Beaumont. Jack Hayward, the Bahamas-based millionaire, lost £35,000. Witness and lawyer agreed on a grand total of £250,000 in debts, and Sir David swivelled on his heels to turn his head and stare fixedly at the reporters' benches behind him – a habit he indulged in from time to time.

Bessell had been in temporary hiding in Mexico while his father-in-law, Miller, negotiated a 17½ per cent settlement with creditors. Sir David: 'There was a greater prospect of getting your creditors to take a token sum if they knew you had disappeared? . . . you designedly kept yourself incommunicado?' Bessell: 'I did until the commencement of negotiations: I thought it would be wiser to let tempers cool – it would give me an opportunity to rehabilitate myself.' No, he went on, his life was not entirely a lie. He then settled in California under his own name, and the local police knew his whereabouts. Anyone who had made a serious attempt to find him could have done so.

But Sir David had already passed on to his bomb-shell. Bessell was due at the time to collect a million-dollar commission for arranging the sale of some of Jack Hayward's American interests. He was in such dire financial straits it was being suggested he might commit suicide. Sir David: 'Did you pretend that if Hayward was willing to pay a bribe of $500,000, it would facilitate the transaction?' Bessell leaned right forward: 'Thorpe and I did so.'

But if he had not done it on his own, why had he written letters saying the contrary? rallied Sir David. Bessell said: 'To protect your client.' He had told the police about the matter the previous week.

Sir David disclosed that Bessell had in fact written a letter to Thorpe containing an 'abject apology'. 'Mr Hayward was one of the major benefactors so far as the Liberal Party was concerned. Are you telling the court that Thorpe was a party to endeavouring to perpetrate a fraud on Hayward?' 'Yes.' Bessell hadn't told Pencourt about it, he said, but he had told his father-in-law and Jack Hayward himself that Thorpe was involved, earlier that year.

Was this one of the matters for which Bessell wanted immunity? No, he had no idea what the immunity was designed to cover. Sir David: 'You weren't interested?' Bessell: 'I suppose that is correct, sir.' How was a personal letter of apology to Thorpe supposed to protect Thorpe? 'To ensure, I hoped it would not embarrass his relationship with Mr Hayward, or cause Hayward to cease to be a benefactor of the Liberal Party.' He wanted Hayward to conclude the whole matter was Bessell's fault.

Sir David then established that Bessell's scheme involved a confirmatory phone call to a 'lady in the US' who was a friend and business associate of Bessell. Sir David: 'But not the person she purported to be on the telephone?' Bessell: 'I do not believe she purported to be anyone other than she was – the purpose was to confirm how much she knew of the negotiations, as I had reported them to Mr Thorpe.' The mysterious phone call was never further explained in court.

Sir David moved to a general conclusion. 'You have . . . succeeded in telling a considerable number of lies over a period of years . . . in some cases to experienced journalists . . . you yourself have said you now have a credibility problem . . . the difficulty is to tell when you are telling the truth and when you are telling lies.' Bessell, with a wry ghost of a smile, said: 'I accept that is the problem.' True, he had discussed with Pencourt how much they made out of their book, although it was not £160,000 as Sir David suggested. Yes, he did hope to make a 'fairly substantial sum' from a book of his own on the affair. He had already got money in advance for serialization rights.

Sir David suddenly went back to detail, and cross-questioned Bessell about his attempts to get Scott work in America. He had deliberately done nothing to get Scott a visa, Bessell conceded, because he was a homosexual, which the Americans would not like, and 'if he went to the United States I would have been likely to have been plagued by him there'. Sir David suggested that when Thorpe supposedly said to Bessell: '"Get rid of him," he was really talking about "get rid of him to America".' Bessell did not agree.

The court ended for the day, and Bessell was driven back to the Castle Hotel at Taunton where he posed for pictures in the lounge, sipping tea out of a china cup. Bessell was not the only one who had had posed pictures arranged. On Tuesday, the second day, Thorpe had taken the unusual step for an accused person of giving the photographers a ten-minute photo facility at his normal lunchtime hotel near the court, in return for them leaving him alone during the rest of the hearing. The following day some photographers arrived – this time hoping to get a photograph of Sir David. But when the Thorpe entourage arrived it was mistakenly assumed the cameramen had broken the agreement and wanted more pictures of him. There was a scuffle and cries of, 'Bastard.' A *Daily Mirror* photographer sent a letter to Thorpe explaining the misunderstanding and on Thursday morning, when the court reconvened for the fourth day, Thorpe marched over to the press benches with an envelope, containing an acceptance of the explanation, which he handed to a reporter to pass on.

It was Bessell's fourth day in the witness box and Sir David had by no means finished. Bessell had sold his story exclusively to the *Sunday Telegraph* for £50,000. 'You've not been wasting any time Mr Bessell, have you?' Bessell was uncomfortable: 'I don't quite follow,' he said. The approach had been made by the newspaper and he had decided to accept.

Sir David tried to clear up one point about the attempted fraud on Jack Hayward. Was it true that he had first mentioned it to the police on the Thursday of the previous week? Yes. 'Because you anticipated I might ask you about it?' – 'Yes, sir.'

It had already been accepted by Bessell that he had changed his story in the spring of 1976, and now Sir David wanted the date more narrowly defined. Bessell repeated he had taken the decision because of representations he had received from members of the Parliamentary Liberal Party.

Sir David said: 'There is an article about you in the *Sunday Times* of 14 March extensively.' Bessell agreed it had embarrassed him. Had he believed Mr Thorpe had assisted in its preparation? 'I thought it was possible Mr Thorpe assisted. I have not pursued the matter as to whether or not I was mistaken.' He added firmly: 'It was not a material factor in deciding to tell my present story.'

He came straight back at Sir David and repeated his assertion when the matter was raised later in the cross-examination. 'I do not think it enraged me as much as another article in the *Sunday Times* on that same date.'

He was not giving evidence at that moment as revenge for the article about him. 'My giving evidence in this case has no connection whatsoever with any article that appeared in the *Sunday Times* about me under the heading "Insight". I may however have been influenced by another article in the *Sunday Times* of the same date headed "The Lies of Norman Scott" by Jeremy Thorpe.'

Sir David turned the clock back to the discussion Bessell claimed to have had with Thorpe and Holmes about murder plans. Bessell had supported Thorpe for the Liberal leadership and campaigned for him, because he thought him the best man for the job. Discussion about murder had only come up after Thorpe had got the leadership. What had Bessell, as a Liberal, done about it? Bessell repeated patiently that he had tried to explain that initially he had not taken it seriously until January 1971, when he and Holmes were in Florida. 'Did you do anything to take out of public life a man who was contemplating murder?' – 'No.' 'That is quite remarkable, isn't it?' – 'I don't think it is, because following the Florida episode it was my view, – and I believe Holmes's view – that the idea had been finally abandoned . . . in retrospect it was undoubtedly irresponsible of me not to have taken some action at that time. The thought crossed by mind but I dismissed it. That is the only answer I can give.'

Bessell emphasized that he had never considered himself bound by any agreement to join in any murder plan. Neither had Holmes. No, there had been no threats, pressure or inducements. 'I wasn't even under persuasion.'

Sir David: 'On the account you give it does not amount to any more than sort of, discussions of possible ways of disposing of Scott.' Bessell replied: 'I think it is an understatement to say it was a discussion only. The fact that there had been the meetings and that Holmes was suggested as the person to carry out the plan meant it was above the "mere discussion stage".'

Sir David read from a copy of *The Pencourt File* to Bessell, what he had told its authors: "'If you look at this whole thing from outside objectively, have you ever heard of a more bungled, stupid, idiotic, childish scheme? I mean, any writer of any penny dreadful can produce a better story than this. And what kind of brain is it that thinks in these terms . . . this notion which is born of *Boys' Own Paper* 1922?'" Bessell chuckled and took off his half-moon spectacles, held round his neck by a thin black cord. 'Those may have been my precise words,' he said.

Sir David moved on to Leonard Ross, the solicitor engaged to handle Scott's divorce. How well did Thorpe know him? Bessell said he thought Thorpe had met him on two or three occasions at board meetings of the companies Bessell and Thorpe were directors of – Manhattan Equipment Ltd, and Drinkmaster Ltd – in Plymouth between 1960 and 1965.

Sir David stopped pecking here and there, and turned to one of his favourite themes – the number of people who had known about Scott's allegations. In 1971, when Bessell and Holmes had been in Florida on the American charade, the following had known: Bessell himself; Holmes; Sir Frank Soskice; Father Sweetman, the Dublin priest; George Thomas MP; Mr David Ennals, while Minister of State at the Health ministry; the solicitor Leonard Ross; the Metropolitan Police Commissioner; Lord Byers, the Liberal Leader in the Lords (Bessell said he did not know that, but had heard so since); and the then Home Secretary, Reginald Maudling. Mr Emlyn Hooson, the Liberal MP, and David Steel, now the Party leader, had known not long after, bringing Sir David's total to twelve.

Sir David pointed out that Bessell had attributed to Thorpe the statement that if the plan worked it was essential that the police should not find letters afterwards. Letters had been purchased from Scott on 25 February 1974. Who had known about the existence of them then? The answer was the following: Bessell's secretaries; Scott himself; Lord Byers; Hooson and his secretary; Steel; some representatives of the Conservative Party; and, of course, the police.

The authors of *The Pencourt File* listened attentively as Sir David embarked on a long cross-examination about their dealings with Bessell.

Bessell agreed that the first possible point of contact with Pencourt could have been not before 13 May 1976 'when they first saw Sir Harold Wilson'. He agreed there had been a series of lengthy transatlantic telephone conversations.

Bessell accepted that he had had a telephone call from Scott some time in June. 'I am suggesting to you the authors of the book and you orchestrated this matter.' Bessell said he was not clear what the purpose of the telephone call had been. Sir David asked him: 'Is it right to say this is the only conversation during the whole of your evidence over ten years about which you cannot remember the particulars?' Bessell replied he could tell the court 'in rough form'. Penrose had told him Scott would like to speak to him because he was depressed. When Scott called, 'all he did was stammer and splutter and say he was glad to speak to me again and that I had been kind to him in the past. He was sorry I was ill . . . I think I asked him what he was doing. To the best of my recollection he talked to me a bit about horses. I would say that was the only purpose and content of the call. I tried to phone back, but the number was out of order.' Sir David, who looked at Bessell with the air of a man experiencing grave distaste, raised a laugh in court as he rejoined: 'Was that because *you* were depressed?'

Sir David became apparently annoyed at Bessell's answers. Bessell insisted that had been the end of the matter and said he thought the purpose of the call was to see how the two men reacted to each other on the telephone. Surely, Sir David said, there was more to it than that – it was not to see if sparks came out of the instrument? 'I suspected what was happening was that someone was going to tape the conversation,' Bessell said.

Sir David then produced a letter written by Bessell to Scott on 13 July 1976, a month later. Bessell examined a copy carefully. Sir David read him a passage in which Bessell said a friend of his, Paul B. Edwards, formerly public relations officer for the United Nations Children's Fund in New York, was coming to Devon from California and would like to see Scott. He was one of the few people who had helped Bessell after his 'world collapsed' in 1974 and would be bringing a memorandum which contained a number of things Bessell would like Scott to know and could be passed on to him in confidence. '"I think they will greatly relieve your mind,"' the letter explained. Sir David described the letter as Bessell 'moving on to Scott's side of the camp'. The unfortunate pun did not go unnoticed on the press benches.

Sir David said shortly: 'Explain.' Bessell said: 'I cannot at the moment remember,' and Sir David set out to turn the knife. 'Is it not significant that despite all the detail you can remember over ten years this has gone from your mind?' Bessell replied that he had had ample opportunity for careful thought and preparation and it was not at all remarkable that he could remember circumstantial detail going back such a long time. But he had been in the witness box for four days. 'I am not saying I am distressed, but at the end of a period like this, when I am doing my best to assist the court, inevitably there will be matters on which my memory may temporarily fail me.' Anyway, he said, Edwards had never got to Devon to see Scott. He was not even sure whether the memorandum had actually been written. Sir David rounded off. 'You acknowledged yesterday you are an accomplished teller of untruths?' Bessell: 'Last night I accepted it was difficult to know when I was telling the truth. You, sir, are a most experienced advocate. I had overlooked to add that in this court I am under oath and what I have said here is the truth –'

he looked towards Thorpe and paused ' – as your client
is well aware.'

Sir David sat down. Taylor conducted a brief re-
examination. He wanted Bessell to be quite clear about
the House of Commons conversations when Holmes
was present. Bessell said: 'The plan to dispose of Mr
Scott was not raised merely as a matter of discussion,
but as a serious proposal addressed to Holmes, for
which purpose he had been invited to London.'

There was the letter Bessell had written to Scott. Sir
David had described it as 'moving into the opposite
camp'. What would be Bessell's way of expressing it?
'My way would be – having consideration for all that
was happening at that time – and the attempt of covering up the truth, that I had a plain responsibility to the
Liberal Party and, indeed, to myself to do everything in
my power to ensure that the matter was finally cleared
up.'

Taylor pointed out to the magistrates that the prosecution had not intended to use the letter, but they
were now legally allowed to do so as a short extract had
been introduced by Sir David in his cross-examination.
He picked up a copy and read it out to the court:

'PO Box 1245
'Oceanside
'California
'July 13 1976

'Dear Norman,
'I was glad to get your letter, I tried to telephone you about
ten days ago but was told your number was out of order. I
wanted to thank you for telephoning me, it was good to hear
your voice again. We have all been through a searing experience and I can imagine how much worse it has been for you in
the midst of it.
[There follows a brief discussion of the coverage in the
papers.]
'From the moment when Newton cum Keane [Andrew
Gino Newton, the gunman who adopted the alias of Keane]
took you on the moor nothing could prevent the facts from

emerging. Although the whole truth has still to be revealed in the fullness of time it will come out. It is one of the tragedies of this saga that none of us are totally without blame. From 1965 onwards it was my first concern to protect Jeremy, as he asked me to do, from any form of public scandal.

'At the same time, as you have recognized, I was genuinely concerned about you and wanted to find ways of helping you. I was very moved by some of the kind things you said about me to the papers. At the beginning of this year when I agreed to Jeremy's final cover-up plan I did you a grave injustice.

'I do not know if anyone told you that on February 8 I wrote to Barnes withdrawing the letter I sent him at Jeremy's and David Holmes's request. This was not, I think, published anywhere. When the full facts began to emerge I realized that I could not allow myself to be used to try to "cover up" such diabolical conduct.

'Weeks after the Newton trial I read your comment in the witness box when you were asked if you had blackmailed me. You said: "Mr Bessell in the end will tell the truth." I admit, Norman, that your faith in me as expressed by that reply brought tears to my eyes. Eventually, as you know, I did tell the truth.

'Tom Mangold (the BBC television reporter) made a ninety-minute film but it was not shown because Jeremy resigned before he could even get it back to England. Now I am told it is locked in a BBC vault where no doubt it will remain.

'However, there are other ways of setting the record straight and as I told you on the telephone I am determined that all the facts shall be brought into the open. Be patient for a little while and you will eventually find peace. . . .

' . . . There are a number of things I would like you to know and which it would not be wise to put in a letter. I am going to let Paul [Edwards[have a memorandum and he can pass these things onto you in confidence. I think they will greatly relieve your mind.

[The letter congratulates Scott on becoming a father again and explains how Bessell's children stood by him. It says he is 'greatly blessed' by his [Bessell's] wife and how they have talked about Scott a lot. At one time she sympathized with Thorpe but although she is desperately sorry for him she realizes how much Scott has suffered and sends her warm regards.]

'I cannot understand what happened to Jeremy's mind at

the end. The greatest shock to me was his statement in the *Sunday Times* of March 14. His categorical denial of any knowledge of things which he not only knew about but in many instances instigated was bad enough.

'But his attack upon you must have shaken many, many people. Strong, secure and powerful men do not attack their fellow humans in that way. It was an act of fear and weakness which did more than anything else to persuade me that, in your words, "in the end" I would have to tell the truth.

'I can understand how you feel about having another dog. Although I do not share your love of horses (I am not a good rider and have never really tried to "come to terms" with them!) I do share your love of dogs. Our three Dachshunds are adorable and you would go crazy over them. Of course, they are totally spoiled and even allowed to sleep with us, which would probably disgust most people.

'You say you are grateful Norman. I cannot think what you have to be grateful to me about. I did you a serious injustice in the beginning of this year and although I have since tried to put it right – and intend to put it completely right, I added to your suffering. I am grateful to you for your understanding.

'The important thing is that we must all be willing to face the absolute truth even if the consequences are not entirely pleasant for any of us. If we are prepared to do this we shall in the end be judged fairly and what more can we ask?

'There is a wonderful side to Jeremy's character which I shall always admire and hold in affection. That does not excuse his actions in respect of you – or for that matter in respect of me – but he needs understanding and sympathy just as much as the rest of us.

'The higher one climbs the ladder the greater the fall. It is important to guard against bitterness. I have found it difficult to do this sometimes and I know you must have had the same struggle. But it only hurts or destroys ourselves if we allow it to overcome us.

'Write to me again soon. I shall look forward to your letters. God bless you.

> 'My warmest regards,
> 'PETER.'

Taylor had one more question.

'Is your evidence true?' 'It is, sir. I agreed with Sir

David that I have told a number of lies over a number of years. I have never lied on oath.'

The court relaxed as Bessell sat down. That afternoon as he went through the laborious process of verifying his eighty-two-page deposition, the defendants all had to stay in court, and Thorpe hàd a brief cat-nap. His wife Marion and his mother used the afternoon to go shopping. The lawyers were hastily revising the provisional time-table for what now looked like marathon proceedings. It was not until well into the next morning that Bessell finally finished checking every page and the next witness was able to take the stand.

4

Hayward and Dinshaw

Jack Hayward, a cheery British millionaire, had flown
in from the Bahamas to be the second witness, and was
holding an impromptu press conference in the court-
room driveway as Peter Bessell went through his depositions.

Hayward, in characteristically sprightly mood, told
reporters clustered round him: 'I'm very anxious to get
back to the Bahamas. I've got some urgent business
there.' Smiling hugely, he disclosed he was due to take
part in a Christmas pantomime, *Aladdin*, and had to
learn the part of Abanazar, the evil magician. 'I wanted
to be Widow Twankey, but they wouldn't let me.' The
journalists wrote down 'Abanazar'. 'It rhymes with
"have a banana",' Hayward said helpfully.

'Union Jack' Hayward was a well-known figure to
reporters. Son of the chairman of Firth Cleveland
Engineering, he settled in the Bahamas after the war,
building up the 'Grand Bahama Development Company'. His fondness for Britain is legendary, and he has
given away more than £500,000 to assorted British
causes. He bought Lundy Island for the nation for
£150,000 when it was in danger of being sold abroad.
He supported the restoration of Brunel's iron steam-
ship the ss *Great Britain*, which had been rotting in the
Falkland Islands. Chay Blyth, the British round-the-
world yachtsman, and women's cricket have benefited
from his generosity. 'Men are better than women,' he
confided this morning, 'but that makes me sound like a
male chauvinist pig.' Hayward, who had patriotically

flown in on the Laker Skytrain from New York, was asked how he felt about his various British good causes. 'I'm glad I supported them,' he said. 'I'm not so sure about other things – you can't win them all.' Sensing his moment, a BBC man thrust his microphone forward. Did he mean that he would not want to contribute any more to British political causes? Hayward's lawyer stepped forward promptly to stop him replying. Answering more harmless questions, such as the date of his birth ('1923, the year Wolverhampton Wanderers were founded'), he was shepherded away to pose for pictures with an Exmoor pony in the adjoining field. Then, at last, he was called into the witness box.

The purpose of calling Hayward was to hear evidence about money – specifically money he had given to the Liberals. The bulk of his testimony came, not so much in what he said in the box, but in his verification of letters Thorpe had written to him.

Hayward first met Jeremy Thorpe in 1969 over the purchase of Lundy Island. Thorpe had been one of the West Country MPs concerned about the issue. A little while later, about eight years ago, he had met Peter Bessell in New York. It was Bessell who had convinced him he should also donate to Liberal Party funds. In 1970 Hayward made a £150,000 gift to the Liberals and received a letter of thanks from the late Sir Frank Medlicott, then party treasurer.

Taylor was really interested in further money Hayward had given to the Liberals around the crucial 1974–5 period. He produced the first of six letters from the pile in front of him and handed it to Hayward to verify. All were hand-written by Thorpe on House of Commons notepaper. The first read:

'April 10 1974

'My dear Jack

'Welcome home! You will want a little time to recover after your journey and I leave for North Devon Thursday April 11, until April 21. We will talk on the telephone but a short letter will probably be helpful by way of background.

'1. – Kissinger – We had an extremely useful and friendly talk at the American Embassy. I gave him a full brief and he has shown definite interest. He wants to contact me again and still wants me to lunch with him in Washington. Ironically, I had a session with Nixon at the reception following Pompidou's memorial service, but did not think I could quite raise Freeport on that occasion! I will give you more news on this when we meet. I am hopeful.

'2. – Bessell – He is a bastard. I do not think there are assets but I will do whatever I can to minimize the damage to you.

'3. – The election – To go from two million to six million was fantastic but we have now got (a) to concentrate relentlessly on the seats where we are a good second, plus (b) try to get up to nine to ten million next time. That would then produce a total breakthrough. Your extremely generous contribution of £50,000 made it possible for me to have a close-circuit TV which enabled me to sew up North Devon for good whilst doing a national TV campaign; paid for the posters, some of the press advertising and helped raise a number of candidates.

'Interestingly, out of 51-plus only 21 polled less than 12 per cent plus and lost their deposit, compared with 28 lost deposits for the Labour Party! We raised a lot more, thank God.

'However, I am now being asked to pay the bills for which I take responsibility and would now be ready and grateful for some help. Delicately, I would like to ask you for two cheques! My reason is this. Each candidate is limited to a total sum for his individual campaign. If he exceeds it by one penny he can be unseated!

'In my case I fought a national and a local campaign from Barnstaple. There is, therefore, an overlap on some expenditure which I would prefer not to have to argue about!

'Accordingly, Nadir Dinshaw, who is Rupert's [Thorpe's son] godfather and who is conveniently resident in Jersey, has agreed to settle bills which fall into this ambiguous category.

'Accordingly, it would be immensely helpful if you could send me two cheques, one for £40,000 for the Liberal Party General Election Fund, and £10,000 payable to Nadir Dinshaw. I can then clear up everything safely.

'Marion and I leave for Canada on April 22 for a Liberal leaders' meeting with Trudeau, and will be back on April 29.

69

Up to April 21 I shall be at Higher Chaggaton, Cobbaton, North Devon. The political situation is very exciting although the possibilities place an awesome responsibility on one. But no complaints!

'My love to Jean (plus the donkeys). And thank you for your munificent and welcome help which really did help to tip the balance.

'Yours ever, Jeremy.'

Hayward duly paid the money in two parts, he said. He transferred £40,000 to the 'Liberal Party General Election Fund', sent to Lloyds Bank at Finsbury Circus in London. On 3 May 1974 he also sent £10,000 to Barclays Bank in Haywards Heath, by a cheque drawn on his company, Protocol Trading Corporation (Exuma) Limited. The cheque was payable to Mr Nadir Dinshaw. It was endorsed on the back by Dinshaw in favour of 'Mourant du Feu and Jeune'.

Thorpe wrote to Hayward eleven days later:

'May 14 1974

'My dear Jack
[He thanks Hayward for his 'munificent and magnificent help' and says the number of seats at the election was a bitter disappointment.]

'Our target now is 600 candidates plus 9 million voters and if this doesn't bust through we shall just have to get ½ million to withhold taxes until they are taken to judgement and/or the system is changed!! You may have seen that we took over the opposition front bench twice last week. I felt rather at home there!

'It was great to see you both at Orme Square [Thorpe's Bayswater home]. My only regret is that we both and in particular you should have been subjected to a dose of Bessellitis. *Damn* the man.
[He thanks Hayward again and tells him to look after the donkeys.]

'Yours as ever. Jeremy.'

Mr Taylor then picked up the next letter dated that autumn and read it out:

'November 28 1974

'Personal and Confidential
'My dear Jack

'It was great seeing you both the other day although for obvious reasons we couldn't talk. My main reason for writing this long overdue letter is to say that I was horrified and shocked – '

Taylor was suddenly interrupted by the bushy-eyebrowed clerk, Fred Winder, who had risen from his seat and was pointing towards the back of the court. Everybody in the court followed his finger and the slight figure of Mr Bessell was discovered sitting on a small bench reserved for the police, close to Mr Thorpe, but out of Hayward's vision.

Taylor said that the Crown wanted Bessell to leave. He got up from his seat and slid out of the court door. Taylor started reading the letter again:

'– I was *horrified* and *shocked* to hear of the extent to which that bastard Bessell landed you in the cart. [Suppressed laughter in court.] I knew of the £10,000 guarantee and hoped perhaps naïvely that it might not be called in but the rest is too ghastly for words.

'I personally feel very much responsible as you would not have met him but for me. If I was a rich man I would send you a cheque for the whole damn lot and try to forget the incident where frankly we were both taken for a ride. Would to God I'd never let him touch the Freeport project and I started with Kissinger at the very beginning.

'The whole thing has sickened me and could have undermined our friendship. It is for me a great blessing that it has not. At least that is a head of damage which he has not inflicted! In view of this, I feel very reluctant to follow up your generous agreement to help. I will set out the facts and if you think enough is enough then God knows I shall understand. [The letter again lays out Liberal election successes and says some Tories, including Du Cann and Whitelaw, are convinced the Liberals 'are here for good'.]

'Eight of us are going to see those companies which have been the Tory Party's chief backers *financially* and suggest that they pressurize the Tories to come round in favour of electoral reform by the next GE.

'(a) Since it would mean that there would never again be a Socialist majority in its own right and (b) it gives Liberals next time a powerful incentive to return a Tory MP where no Liberal is standing or where his chances are remote. Marks and Spencer are the first converts! Once we get the system changed then we go into coalition since we'll have over 100 plus, possibly 150 MPs. [Hayward is thanked again for his donations. Thorpe says the Party raised £300,000 independently of the constituencies.]

'When I rang you I was £40,000 short and you generously said you would meet half if I raised half but to come back rather than sail the ship. In fact, the total needed went up to £42,000 but I raised £25,000 so I am still needing to raise £17,000. With that all election bills can be settled. If, with incredible generosity, you felt disposed to close the gap, I should be immensely grateful. But if you say you've been Bessellized and that's that, well then I shall understand although will be bloody pushed!

'. . . Damn the swine. He's cost me a little but that was at least an honourable transaction . . .

'Am helping poor old Constantine to win his referendum. I fear he'll miss it but his TV performance (recorded here and sent out to Greece) was I gather brilliant and he's gaining ground. It may turn on what help Makarios gives him when the old fox goes to Athens. Never had a King for a candidate before.

'Have a great Christmas. If you remember buy a Dinky car for me to put in old Wal's stocking.

'Yours ever. Jeremy.'

Thorpe had not written again until the next year, when he sent this letter:

'March 5 1975

'My dear Jack

'I hope you all flourish. I thought of you during the Queen's visit and hoped you would not have been regarded as too white to be asked to the Receptions! From all accounts the visit seems to have been a triumph but still the bloody Left go on grousing about the cost of the monarchy, which is slightly less than the cost of running the British Embassy in Paris!

'Marion and I went to a fabulous party at the Palace last month (the day after Margaret Thatcher had been elected, with poor Ted there!).

[Thorpe talks about a holiday in Africa during which he met Kenyatta, 'a fabulous old boy', and went on a fact-finding visit to Rhodesia, during which he saw Ian Smith and 'all the African Nationalists'.]

'I compiled a very full report for Callaghan and the three African Presidents and received a request for a copy from the Monarch! So at least they are all informed. Not much hope. Vorster is trying.

'I got a copy of the letter from Mr Fred Miller of New York which seemed to show a slight improvement in affairs. Where and when Bessell will surface I know not, but I certainly hope that he will seek to make amends.

'Politics are taking an interesting turn. The Government are hopelessly split on Europe and on the Social Contract. Margaret Thatcher is far more amenable than Heath. I could do business with her. At present we are canvassing the twenty-four companies who were the major subscribers to the Tory Party. [He explains again the argument they are putting to them.]

'You have done more than any one man (with the possible immodest exception of myself!!!) to keep the Liberal Party alive and see it climb to the five to six million mark. I have therefore done all I could to keep down GE expenses but now the bills are coming in. I asked if you could manage £17,000 since this coupled with other money raised (£25,000 Weinstock, £25,000 Geoffrey Edwards and others) will enable me just to break even.

'If you were so disposed, a cheque could be made payable to the Liberal Election Fund but, ideally, since some expenditure could just conceivably held by my opponents to be attributable to the North Devon campaign – although the fact is it was almost wholly national expenditure – and since I can be *unseated* if I pay bills which result in me exceeding the permitted total – it would be safest if we could repeat the February 74 procedure and make £10,000 payable to Jeune Fullerton and Dinshaw, La Rocquaise, St Brelades Bay, Jersey, if possible from an external account. Jeune Fullerton are accountants and Dinshaw is Rupert's godfather. They would then settle bills. The balance could quite safely be paid into UK unless it is easier to do the lot direct to the Channel Islands.

'And now Jack let me give you the good news! I think you have earned a long rest from subscribing to Liberal funds. I can personally never be grateful enough to you for what you have done. If you could manage the request then I should be enormously relieved and grateful. [He tells Hayward to look after himself.]

'Yours as ever, Jeremy.'

The fifth letter followed four months later:

'July 6 1975

'My dear Jack

'Little did you realize . . . after we spoke I offered to go to Uganda and got back a message via the Ugandan High Commission that Amin would see me and welcome a visit. I contacted Callaghan as a matter of courtesy – to be told about the General and the Queen's letter. We both agreed that a visit from me then would be overdoing it! But it was a close one. The man is a dangerous lunatic. [He says the 16 July dinner to celebrate five years of David Steel as Liberal Whip is going ahead.]

'If you could generously manage the £9000 needed for settling the outstanding election bill (through the ordinary UK account) this would help enormously ease a rather pressing situation. The £10,000 external is not so urgent. The first all-party meeting on electoral reform has taken place and things move very hopefully.

'More news anon.

'Yours as ever. Jeremy.'

Taylor then produced a cancelled cheque which Hayward had sent, dated 14 July 1975 and drawn on his company as before. It was for £9000 and made out to the Liberal Party Direct Aid Committee.

The cheque was sent direct to Thorpe.

Thorpe wrote back promptly:

'July 18 1975

'My dear Jack

'You are a kind and generous creature! I am deeply grateful. You cheque has relieved me of quite a few worries which
were beginning to pile up. Thank you with all my heart.
[He says it was lovely to see Hayward at the 16 July dinner
and says the trip to Lundy which they had been trying to
arrange for some time is now definitely on for September.] 'I
am giving a good deal of thought to reactivating the Mobil
deal or a comparable one.

'I think probably this now involves meeting Henry K again
for general discussion – here if he stays over – in Washington
if not. The thing to avoid is to give the impression that we are
rushed. I must say it would help if we had had an inquiry from
Cuba – or worse!

'Anyway leave that one to me for a little. Again Jack my
profound gratitude. You have done as much as any man to
keep us in business and I modestly believe that that has had
some beneficial result for Britain – not least in preventing the
total polarization between the two Giants.

'Love to Jean.

'Yours as ever. Jeremy.'

It was not until 24 November 1975 that Hayward
finally sent the second of his two £10,000 payments to
Jersey. Taken once more from his company, Protocol,
this time it was despatched to 'Messrs Jeune, Fullerton
and Dinshaw' in Jersey.

Taylor questioned Hayward on his dealings with Liberals. The first time Hayward met David Holmes, he
explained, was on a visit to Lundy Island when he, his
wife, Thorpe and Holmes were all there. Had Hayward
ever sought to hide the contributions he made to Liberal Party funds? 'Not as far as I remember. I have
never sought confidential ways of making contributions.' He confirmed: 'It was Thorpe's idea' that the
£10,000 should be paid to Dinshaw.

There was one further point the Crown now wanted
to establish: what had happened more recently as police
had started their investigations. In April 1978, seven

months before the Minehead proceedings opened, Thorpe arranged to see Hayward during one of his London visits at the offices Hayward used in Pall Mall. 'He asked me to put pressure on Bessell for the money he owed me, and threaten that if he came back to this country, I would serve a writ on him for bankruptcy. This was ostensibly to prevent Bessell's return to the United States as he would be an undesirable. . . . He had his girl friend, now his wife, in the United States.' Hayward added grimly: 'I took no action.'

In early May, police rang up Hayward in the Bahamas and asked him about the two payments of £10,000 each that had been sent to Jersey. Hayward rang Thorpe. 'I asked him to remind me about them – why they were sent to Jersey.' Thorpe told him the money had been for election expenses and he gave him the name of the Jersey accountants involved. 'I asked him what it was all about, why the police were investigating, and who was Mr Dinshaw.' Thorpe reminded him he was the godfather of his son Rupert. 'I said: "What has happened?" He made a remark: "Dinshaw has presumably panicked."' Hayward finished his evidence with: 'It left me rather puzzled.'

John Mathew, Holmes's counsel, established that – apart from a letter of thanks for a lunch invitation and a pub lunch in London – Hayward and Holmes had had nothing to do with each other.

Thorpe's lawyer, however, wanted to confront Hayward on a number of points. The cross-examination got off to a slightly less than cordial start. Sir David rose and announced reassuringly that there was no suggestion Hayward himself had any significant knowledge of any of the matters the court was directly concerned with (the conspiracy to murder). 'Thank you very much,' Hayward replied indignantly.

Hayward was not in fact a direct supporter of the Liberal Party, was he? Sir David challenged him. Hayward appeared amazed: 'I think I have been the biggest supporter in their history.' He agreed he did not regard himself as a Liberal or a member of the Liberal Party but Thorpe had persuaded him the Liberals needed private funds. Labour had the unions, the Conservatives big business, and 'the Liberal Party was the underdog'. Hayward was prepared to agree that a significant factor in donating so much money had been Jeremy Thorpe himself, who he had met over the campaign to save Lundy. He agreed: 'I formed a very high opinion indeed of him and his abilities.'

In his testimony Hayward had given Bessell the credit for his original decision to hand over £150,000 to the Liberals in 1970. He now confirmed, at Sir David's request, that Bessell later came to owe him £35,000, including a £10,000 bank guarantee which had been called upon. Hadn't Thorpe himself talked to Hayward about making contributions to Liberal funds in August 1969, on Lundy? Hayward's impression was that no sum had been decided on. 'Mr Bessell was really the emissary of Mr Thorpe.' Sir David pressed on: Bessell's visit was to finalize the earlier mention of £150,000. 'I don't think so. Bessell brought a long memorandum from Sir Frank Medlicott ... as a result of which I settled upon a figure of £150,000. Sir Frank mentioned various amounts which would do various things ... £150,000 would clear all debts and help fight the General Election.'

Sir David took a new tack. He handed Hayward a letter. 'This is addressed to Peter Bessell,' Hayward said. Sir David, directing him to the fourth paragraph, said: 'You were suggesting that donations should not be made public.' He had only meant, Hayward said, that the £150,000 should be kept quiet for the time being in order to stimulate other donations. No, he had not said at a London lunch that he wanted the donation kept quiet out of deference to his father, who would disagree with it. 'He knew of the donation pretty well from the outset. It was in the press.' He agreed he had trusted Thorpe to disburse the later 1974 and 1975 money as he saw fit, for Liberal Party purposes.

Suddenly, as Sir David ploughed on, a note was hastily passed up to the court clerk. With dramatic urgency, the court was cleared – a bomb threat had been phoned in. Everybody filed outside to stand shivering in the chill wind which had replaced the unseasonably balmy weather. Thorpe made a show of looking under his car for the bomb. Then, as everyone jostled together in the yard, he came up against Hayward. He shot out his hand. An obviously startled Hayward grasped it, and each said almost simultaneously: 'I'm not allowed to speak to you,' as a policeman firmly shepherded Thorpe away.

The first week was over, and after five hard days the week-end break was welcomed by everyone involved except Hayward, who had hoped to finish his evidence that afternoon. The press corps split, some taking the opportunity to go back to London whilst others stayed on for a country week-end. The week's work had been exhausting for the reporters who had had to telephone prodigious amounts of copy compared to any usual court case. The daily paper reporters got their normal revenge on their Sunday paper colleagues, watching them going through the tortuous Friday-night process of compiling their only report of the week.

The more experienced, and generous, journalists were already making arrangements for chocolates and cigarettes to be ferried to the hard-pressed GPO switch-board girls struggling to deal with the volume of transfer charge calls every day. The gifts were of course partly out of self-interest – the operators were their lifeline to their offices and, for the evening paper reporters especially, every minute counted.

The reporters found it hard to get away from the story, even though some arranged for wives or girl friends to come down to keep them company. Most of them were getting more in the paper every day than they had ever done in their lives, and the case had become an obsession for them.

The pubs and restaurants echoed every night with

endless discussions and arguments about the virtues of the evidence. One reporter, who had been loudly voicing his opinions about a star witness underneath the oak beams of a popular hotel restaurant, had been extremely embarrassed the next day to realize that the witness had been sitting right behind him as he held forth.

Thorpe went home to do some gardening. He returned with everybody else when Hayward stepped promptly into the witness box at 10 a.m. on Monday morning.

He was not there for long. Sir David asked him: 'You were not anxious to have your private affairs discussed in court?' Hayward looked at him blankly. 'I can't follow you,' he said. Sir David tried again. Hayward: 'Obviously I did not want to appear in court. One prefers not to.' Sir David added rapidly: 'I am not suggesting you have anything to hide.'

Sir David asked him if he remembered asking for anonymity. 'No,' said Hayward. 'I'm not really an anonymous person. I forget a bit about money but I don't forget about anything to do with PR [public relations].'

Obviously exasperated by the questioning, he said: 'The word anonymity is not mentioned in any of Mr Thorpe's letters to me and if it was such a burning issue I feel sure in the many letters, some very lengthy, it would at least have been mentioned and he would have assured me any future donations would have been dealt with discreetly and anonymously.' He added very firmly: 'I must disagree I preferred to be anonymous.'

John Bull, for the prosecution, re-examined very briefly. (Bull, Taylor's junior counsel, was familiar to some reporters as the junior to the prosecution in the 'Operation Julie' LSD trials at Bristol earlier in the year.) Hayward said that his original £150,000 donation had been 'well broadcast'. 'None of this payment was asked to be diverted through Jersey. It went straight to Sir Frank Medlicott,' he said.

As far as the prosecution was concerned, the issue of the money used for the alleged murder plot was a self-contained area. There were only two witnesses, Hayward, and the Jersey-based accountant, Nadir Dinshaw. Theoretically Dinshaw should have come next in the evidence. In fact his comparatively brief testimony was slotted in the following week.

In complete contrast to Hayward, Dinshaw had a dislike of publicity, and was uneasy about appearing in such a sensational spotlight. When he came to the court on the morning of Tuesday 5 December he brought with him a lawyer, Larry Grant, well-known for his civil liberties work. Dinshaw's main job for the prosecution was to sketch in greater detail the payments Hayward had already described. But his evidence was also to provide a surprise which the Crown made much of in the final submission.

Thorpe asked him to hand the Hayward money on to David Holmes, Dinshaw explained. He was to keep the transaction confidential. The money was for election expenses. Dinshaw said he had been reassured after the second request, in autumn 1974, that there was to be no question of publicity for his role in the matter. 'I was rather unhappy about having to do it again. I stressed I didn't want any kind of publicity. I knew Mr Hayward had had unpleasant publicity early on.' The second £10,000 had been passed over to Holmes in cash sums of about £500 a time. This was Holmes's idea. It was also Holmes's idea that Dinshaw should start handing over the money in advance of Hayward's November cheque from the spring of 1975.

Alarm overcame Dinshaw when he was watching the television news in March 1976. It said that Holmes had paid £2500 for some letters. He went to the Dean of Westminster, Dr Edward Carpenter, and told his old friend the whole story. He also told David Steel, the Liberal MP. By this time, Dinshaw had handed over £7500 in cash to Holmes, but Holmes assured him it had not been used for the letters. The first Hayward money had come in May 1974, while Holmes bought the letters two months earlier.

Taylor turned to later conversations Dinshaw had had after October 1977 when Jeremy Thorpe had held a press conference in the National Liberal Club [about the dog shooting and Scott's claims]. 'I felt very sorry for the horrible way in which he'd been treated,' Dinshaw said. Thorpe rang him in Jersey, and arranged a London lunch the following Thursday. Why had Dinshaw paid the Hayward money to Holmes? '"Because you told me to,"' Dinshaw answered Thorpe. Thorpe suggested that Dinshaw could say he had given the money to Holmes himself. '"Certainly not – how can I say a thing like that? In any case, the money has come from Jack Hayward. The bank accounts will show it."' Thorpe said they wouldn't look at the bank accounts except in criminal matters – '"This is a criminal matter."' Then Thorpe suggested Dinshaw ought to explain the money did come from Hayward, but 'as part of a business deal'. He wouldn't know Jack Hayward if he walked into the room, Dinshaw said – '"How could I say a thing like that in any case?"' Thorpe was obviously very distressed. 'He said it would be very awkward for him.' He had loaned David Holmes some of the money – 'David had needed it very badly.' Pressed by Dinshaw, he said it was £5000.

Dinshaw, grasping the witness box and leaning forward, said he had urged Thorpe to tell the truth. 'I stress I didn't for one moment think he had any part in any conspiracy to murder. I said I thought he'd been very cruelly treated by the press.' 'He said it would be very awkward for *me* if I was asked why I paid the money in cash, but I said: "I must tell the truth." He said it would be very awkward publicity-wise in the context of my desire not to have any publicity.'

The next day Thorpe rang again. Holmes had been spoken to and 'everything was all right and above board'. What had Holmes then done with the money?

'He [Thorpe] said he didn't think any useful purpose would be served by telling me.'

By the next April, six months later, Hayward and Dinshaw's names were being mentioned in the press. Thorpe rang again and took Dinshaw for a drive in St James Park, Westminster. When he brought up the subject of the money, Dinshaw cut him short, saying: '"Well Jeremy, I told you I have to tell the truth about that."'

'Thorpe replied: "Yes, quite so, but if I could only *get* the £20,000, I could say: 'That's the money.'" "Don't be ridiculous: how can you say that's the money when I paid it to David Holmes between 1974 and 1976?"'

It would be very awkward for him, Thorpe said: there were people out to destroy him. He didn't know what happened to the £20,000. (Dinshaw commented this was not what he had been told the previous November.) Thorpe announced to Dinshaw that his political career would be over. '"What does that matter? You have to clear yourself of a possible charge of conspiracy."'

'"I'm not worried about that."' Thorpe was bothered about his political career, talked about Hayward suing him, and about trying to find money to repay him. The following Tuesday, 18 April, Thorpe rang again, apparently a little calmer. 'He said he quite understood my position, but I need not tell more than I was asked – I presume to the police.' Dinshaw was due to see the police himself the following Friday and was highly upset about the unwelcome publicity. Thorpe told him: '"It will be curtains for me and you will be asked to move on."' This 'crude threat', Dinshaw said, presumably meant he would have to leave Jersey or the UK. After a slight tangle about the exact words Dinshaw had uttered in the witness box, the clerk carefully read into the depositions: 'It was a threatening remark which I didn't take at all seriously because it was such a foolish one.' The Karachi-born business man, with his heavy olive face and conservative dark-blue striped suit, repeated his final words to Thorpe: 'I said I would tell the truth.'

Holmes's counsel extracted a few more details of the way the cash went to Holmes. Holmes would ring up in Jersey saying, when Dinshaw was next in London, would he bring a little more money. It was handed over either at the Chesterfield Hotel, where Dinshaw stayed, or at the Reform Club. There had been no receipts. 'I always trust my friends.'

Sir David Napley did not have much to ask on Thorpe's behalf. Dinshaw confirmed Thorpe was apparently 'not in the least concerned about' the criminal charge. It was the political implications that had worried him. 'I remember saying it was far better to be thought of as careless in financial matters than being involved in a conspiracy to murder.'

5

Andrew Gino Newton

The arrival of Andrew Gino Newton, the supposed bungling hit-man, brought the proceedings abruptly down to earth after the high finance and politics. It was to be the subject of some sarcasm later by the defence. He roared up the road to the court at high speed in his metallic blue Opel and swung abruptly into the court entrance, narrowly missing some eager photographers. They were astonished to see that the windows of the car had been specially darkened, and that Newton had put a balaclava helmet over the bottom of his face so that only a pair of eyes was visible.

He was late.

Newton was in a unique position in that he had already been convicted for shooting Scott's dog, Rinka, when he was jailed for two years at Exeter Crown Court on 19 March 1976. Newton's story at that trial had been that Scott had been blackmailing him and he had backed this up with much circumstantial detail. His sentence was for 'carrying a firearm with intent to endanger life'. He had been adamant that at no time had he had any intention of harming Scott. All he had wanted was to frighten him enough to make him give back the nude picture Newton claimed he was being blackmailed about.

Meanwhile, in the court-room, after Hayward had finished reading back his depositions, Bull tidied up loose ends by reading uncontested written statements. One was by Ross, the London solicitor who had acted for Scott in his divorce proceedings. He said he had not brought the subject of Scott's alleged relationship wth Thorpe into the proceedings after speaking to solicitors for Scott's wife, who said it did not come into the divorce. Scott then told him he did not wish Ross to continue to act for him, and he had received a cheque for £77.55 for his fees. 'I believe it was signed by Mr Thorpe,' he said.

By this time Newton had got himself sorted out and strode into the court, a stocky figure with a receding hairline and a small moustache. His loose Aran-knit sweater contrasted sharply with the formal wear of the previous witnesses and practically everyone else in court.

He stood cheerfully in the witness box, looking round the court and peering at various people; he chose to affirm rather than take the oath.

He confirmed he lived at Abinger Road, Chiswick, London, and in 1975 had been a pilot with British Island Airways, living in St Anne's, Lancashire. He said he had gone to the Showman's dinner in Blackpool on 26 February of that year with his friend David Miller, who lived in Cardiff. He had known him for twelve years since they had been students at Chiswick Polytechnic. During the dinner he had met George Deakin, and asked if it was true he wanted somebody 'bumped off'. '"I'm your man,"' he told Deakin, who showed casual interest.

But when he met Deakin again, at Miller's silk-screen printing works a few weeks later, the proposition was put forward once more. This time, money was discussed. 'It was said £15,000 would be the price.' A couple of weeks after that, he arranged to meet Deakin at Aust service station, on the M4 near the Severn Bridge. The two sat in Deakin's car in the car park. Deakin had a catalogue of photographs of Scott lying between the two front seats. He had not touched it but pointed to it, and said that was the gentleman 'who had to be disposed of'. 'He named the town of Dunstable. I knew where it was.'

Taylor asked him if he'd asked questions. 'I asked the normal questions you would expect a professional hit man to ask,' said Newton helpfully. Taylor decided to make his point clear. 'What do you mean by a professional hit man?' Newton was at a loss for a second, and then he replied, 'Somebody who gets renumiation [remuneration] for killing somebody.' Deakin had only given him a loose answer when he asked who wanted the killing done – '"someone else wants it done"' – and told him the sum had come down to £10,000. It was to be paid 'after the deed had been done in cash'.

Newton explained how on his next days off he went to Dunstable to try to find Scott. He tried the library, looking in telephone directories, and the electoral register. When he'd exhausted the area, he telephoned Deakin again. Deakin suggested he deal direct with the person concerned. 'He gave me the name Holmes, and the phone number in Manchester. I did not know who Holmes was.'

Newton rang Holmes up and established that Scott was in fact in Barnstaple, not Dunstable. He said, with unconscious dryness: 'In view of the error, it was suggested I deal direct and have a meeting to prohibit any mistakes being made. It was my idea.'

Holmes and he agreed to meet at the Royal Court Hotel in Sloane Square. Newton identified himself by wearing a red anorak. The two discussed matters over coffee. 'Holmes said it was agreed – £10,000. My brief was that I should kill Norman Scott, and when I asked him how he wanted Norman Scott disposed of, he replied he would prefer it if he vanished from the face of the earth and was never to be seen again. It was left to me how to do it.'

Newton then described the first of his bungled plans. He rang Scott up and told him he was a representative of an Italian company, the Pinserio Group, who were interested in employing him as a model. Scott was invited to come to London and stay at the Royal Gar-

86

den Hotel, Kensington, where they could meet and discuss terms. 'He seemed quite excited. I recall £600 was to be paid.'

Newton's planned disposal method was rather bizarre. 'I bought a chisel and some flowers. The chisel was to bend over his head. I was going to kill Norman Scott.' The prosecution then handed to him a ten-inch chisel, its grey paint virtually intact. He confirmed it was the one. 'I put it with the rest of my tools in my shed at the bottom of the garden at my mother's house. Its other purpose was to break some bricks up.'

Reporters on the press benches exchanged astonished looks, and Taylor asked, with a trace of humour in his voice: 'Which were you going to do first?' 'I think I was going to do Norman Scott first,' Newton replied, grinning and looking round the court. Realizing he was being a little too jokey, he said, apparently to himself: 'This is a serious matter, I know.'

He explained that the flowers were bought to conceal the chisel when he went into the hotel. Scott had not turned up. 'I breathed a sigh of relief. I asked myself on many occasions what I would have done.' Taylor asked him: 'At the time you bought the chisel, had you the intention to kill him?' Newton replied: 'Yes.'

He got in touch with Holmes, who said: '"Leave it to me."' The next plan was made by Holmes. He rang up, and said he had arranged for Scott to go to the Holiday Inn at Bristol to be interviewed by a reporter by the name of 'Matheson'.

Taylor asked him how it was spelt. Newton looked straight across at Holmes, sitting immaculately opposite him, and said: 'I suggest you ask David Holmes.' Holmes smiled slightly, and there was laughter in court. Newton was obviously having difficulty remembering the sequence of events and said: 'I think something is left out here,' but he forged on as best he could.

Scott did not turn up at the Holiday Inn, either. 'I was anxious to get the reins back and to be in control of the situation. I said: "Leave this matter to me." ' His next move was to go down to Barnstaple in a hired yellow Mazda, where he waited in the Pannier Market until Scott came along carrying his laundry. He accosted him and said, '"I want to talk to you about this blackmail."' 'He broke out in a cold sweat.' Scott turned down his idea of a ride in the car but suggested a drink. 'He poured his heart out to me concerning his life, his pathological hatred of the Liberal Party, his dislike for Jeremy Thorpe and anything connected with the Liberal Party.' Scott showed him letters on House of Commons notepaper and produced a lot of documentary evidence. He thought he was being poisoned by a doctor. 'He was writing a book and eating tablets two by two. I said I was being paid by a woman to protect him. There was no truth in this.'

Newton wrote down everything Scott told him on the back of one of his pink airline duty rostas. Newton explained what had been going on in his head at the time. 'I was trying to win his confidence to indirectly get him on his own and bungling a murder attempt. I knew too much already and I could not simply frighten Scott without putting my position in danger with the conspirators.' The plan was to tell them afterwards that the gun had jammed and Norman Scott had managed to run away. 'I could simply say I had tried to kill him but he was able to identify me and they would have to find someone else.'

Newton told Scott he was being paid to protect him from a fictitious Canadian who was coming across to England to kill him.

He then went back to Blackpool and met Holmes by W. H. Smith's at Piccadilly station in Manchester. He told Holmes he had seen the letters for which somebody had paid £2500. Holmes replied: '"Oh Christ,"' and asked what documents there were, and who was mentioned in the conversations. 'I told him I had seen letters, photostats and originals, from Jeremy Thorpe. He asked a lot of questions.' Holmes told him he and

Deakin had tried to steal Norman Scott's briefcase on a previous occasion. 'That's why I thought it was black-mail,' Newton explained.

On 24 October, the day of the shooting finally came. Newton was equipped with a Mauser .32 automatic and eight bullets he had borrowed from an old school friend, Dennis Meighan. (Meighan, who had minor previous convictions, told the court in a statement that antique firearms were his hobby. Newton had said he was being blackmailed and wanted to frighten some-one.)

There had been one mishap already: ringing Scott to arrange a meeting, Newton had forgotten his alias. He introduced himself on the phone as 'Andrew', hastily changing it to '"And you."' As Scott said uncom-prehendingly: '"What?"' on the other end, Newton finally came up with: '"How are you?"' Then a second thing went wrong. Scott turned up for the rendezvous 'with an enormous dog', telling Newton he had only to click his fingers and it would tear his throat out. Newton decided to go ahead just the same. He dropped Scott off briefly at the village of Porlock on the Somerset coast, making an excuse he had to see someone, while he considered this new problem.

He picked Scott up again and drove him on to the cliff tops, where he shot the dog dead, and pointed the gun at Scott. The safety catch was on, he told the court, and he was pretending it was jammed. Scott 'just froze like a sausage'. Driving to Cardiff, and his friend Mil-ler's, Newton then explained he had pretended to re-pair the gun there. 'He obliged me with a screwdriver, pliers and some rags.'

His memory jogged by counsel, Newton now flapped his hands exasperatedly and eventually recalled he had telephoned Deakin from Heathrow Airport. He told him: '"I've seen Scott, tried to shoot him and the gun jammed."'

Newton now recounted a series of six meetings he had with David Holmes, while on bail awaiting trial for

the dog-shooting (the police had soon picked him up).
Scott's Barnstaple landlady, Mrs Friendship, noted the
number of the hired Mazda Newton once arrived in.
This was Scott's idea, she was to testify later.

Newton met Holmes at St Peter's Church in Bolton;
at Manchester Victoria station; at London Paddington
station, where they talked on the phone from adjoining
kiosks and Newton got £300; at London Euston station, where he got another £100; and at a pancake
house in Chelsea. Holmes seemed concerned about the
false blackmail story Newton had concocted all on his
own. '"He said he was going to America with a view to
helping my alibi."' A letter would be sent substantiat-
ing the story to 'a friend of the court'.

Once again, Newton lost track in the series of 'What
happened next?' questions from the Crown. 'It's a bit
like I-Spy,' he said plaintively. 'I know that you know
what you want me to say. . . .' There was laughter.

Holmes mentioned Thorpe, at the Manchester Victoria meeting. 'He said important people were
involved.' Holding on to his narrative thread, Newton
explained that it looked to Holmes as if he was going to
prison for six months, and Holmes offered him half the
original contract – £5000.

Newton served more than a year of his sentence in
jail before being paroled in April 1977. He described
the 'meet' on St Brides Common when the £5000 was
handed over by Le Mesurier, accompanied by Miller.
There was a 'panic' when Le Mesurier spotted a woman
in a car with a telephoto lens, and he drove off with
Newton beside him into a brick factory yard. 'I didn't
know whether I was going for a "halo count" myself,'
Newton said. With a gun in his jacket, he ordered Le
Mesurier to keep his hands on the wheel. Le Mesurier
gave him an envelope, saying: '"There's five Gs in there
from people in London."' 'They wanted to be sure I
was going to keep quiet, and would I oblige?'

Newton announced he wanted a job as well. '"No
problem,"' Le Mesurier told him. The money, in used

mixed notes, was later recovered in part from its hiding place in a tubular deck chair in his mother's house in Chiswick, West London, and Peter Taylor now handed across a large brown envelope for Newton to inspect. As he fingered the plastic bundles inside, Newton's jokiness got the better of him. 'Do you mind if I leave now, as well?' he said to Taylor, giving him a weak grin. Donati, the chairman of the Bench, and Taylor both stared blankly at him. The photographs of the St Brides Common 'meet' on 18 April 1977 were handed over. Yes, said Newton, there was Miller, Le Mesurier and himself, in a red anorak again.

At this point in the events, Newton had got hold of a tape-recorder and attached it to his telephone. He taped calls between himself and Holmes, and between himself and Le Mesurier. Newton said: 'The conversations were about positive proof of conspiracy to murder.' Later in the proceedings, material from Newton's phone conversation with Holmes was read into the evidence.

To make this and other transcripts sound sensible when the time came to read them, the two Crown lawyers undertook a bizarre charade. Standing side by side in their black coats and striped trousers, like schoolboys delivering a recitation on Speech Day, the two acted out material from them for the magistrates' benefit. Taylor's junior, Bull, would be Newton; and Taylor himself – 'I'm Holmes.' The magistrates peered at him.

There was testimony available from four expert witnesses, Taylor said, that the tapes had been authenticated: the voices belonged to the right people. The Crown only relied on them as evidence against the particular defendant concerned: none of them could implicate Thorpe.

The dialogue went, in part, like this:

NEWTON: '. . . Um look, I have to get a couple of things straight, right? . . . The press right? . . . Now, they have been on to me. . . . Now then, something, somewhere along the line somebody must have said something . . . what about the Sloane Square? Have you, did you tell anybody?'

HOLMES: 'No.'

NEWTON: 'Well what about Dave Miller?'

HOLMES: 'I don't know him.'

NEWTON: 'Yeah well, obviously John does, right?'

HOLMES: '. . . let's stick to my South Wales and your South Wales. My South Wales wouldn't know about that anyway. . . .'

NEWTON: '. . . I've been told from er John that you in fact have had a telephone call . . . it took the form of a threat. . . .'

HOLMES: '. . . Um I know who I was told it was from.'

NEWTON: 'What, MI5?'

HOLMES: 'Hmm. . . . I think they are concerned that, if the whole subject came up again for some, er, weakness on my part, things that happened that I know nothing about and have nothing to do with, any of us could very well appear as well, is my interpretation.'

NEWTON: '. . . there's one person knows the full story, um you know, at my end . . . when I was in the States I got hit by a lorry. . . . It took three blinking attempts to run me over, you know, and I take great exception to this, you know er. . . .'

* * * * * * * * * *

HOLMES: 'You, you you know that in this one, um, one comes up against something called conspiracy which is extremely important to know – a lot of other things and that therefore I would be in exactly the same position and it wouldn't be comfortable. . . . I mean I think it's uncomfortable for all of us and it simply is a question of sitting it out.'

* * * * * * * * * *

NEWTON: '. . . You know Deakin, Dave Miller.'

HOLMES: 'Don't produce any names because I never

know about my telephone. . . . I have every reason to be totally silent.'

* * * * * * * * * *

NEWTON: '. . . this isn't no new sort of common knowledge among press men that Sallinger threw a bag of – not a bag – a bundle of notes across to the reporter to turn the story to the South African angle. . . . Well, John was supposed to pass this news on to you.'

HOLMES: 'Perhaps he did. I think I would have probably – if that's some time ago, I would have discounted that because it was so unlike – because he is terribly mean, really.'

* * * * * * * * * *

NEWTON: 'In view of the attempt at . . . me, having a go at me. Now you know, I have got an unnatural and not natural desire to try and stay around a bit longer.'

HOLMES: 'Well, absolute hand on heart, I do assure you that had nothing to do with anyone that I know. . . .'

NEWTON: 'I don't know how long it is going to take to get to Rhodesia but when I go there, I'll certainly make a note of telling somebody. . . . I don't want anything sort of going wrong you know, you see.'

HOLMES: 'It is the last place in the world that there is any English influence.'

NEWTON: '. . . what the press are trying to do . . . they want to tie up with this BOSS angle . . . the South African involvement.'

HOLMES: 'Oh I see.'

NEWTON: 'Because it ties up with Sallinger. The last thing I had, I had some female reporter come and a pair of them came up. Because my name was Nievedonski at one time.'

HOLMES: 'Hum.'

NEWTON: 'They thought I was involved with the KGB. . . .'

HOLMES: 'Come back to the one point, to the central factor in, to you in fact, you have made to me, um that – if you say nothing, I say nothing.'

NEWTON: 'All right.'

HOLMES: 'And they aren't able to prove anything.'

NEWTON: '. . . Remember when we was at Euston station, I said I think somebody has photographed us.'

HOLMES: 'Hum.'

NEWTON: 'Well I don't know, but I think I don't know probably it was you or somebody else but they knew about that.'

HOLMES: 'Let me also ask various friends of mine, who are professionals at this game. I have a photograph showing me talking to one particular great musician that I much admired. He didn't know who I was. He had actually asked me for the time. . . .'

NEWTON: '. . . I think you've had a reporter come round, haven't you, who asked you if you were a friend of er Jeremy Thorpe's and you said no and he came back the next day and you invited him in, is that correct?'

HOLMES: 'No.'

* * * * * * * * * *

NEWTON: 'But what I am trying to get at is that John the Carpet –'

HOLMES: 'Hm yes but.'

NEWTON: '– had suggested that if I go to um Rhodesia.'

HOLMES: 'Stop producing names every conversation, because I mean the whole thing terrifies me. I know who you are talking about, get on. . . .'

NEWTON: '. . . er Miller right I suggest we don't touch him at all.'

HOLMES: 'Yeah OK.'

NEWTON: 'OK um because I think you know his eyes seems to go round like blinking cash registers or fruit machines himself. . . .'

HOLMES: 'I'll make sure that nothing else is ever said . . . and just one thing. If it becomes necessary for us to have any more words, talk via my friend in South Wales don't please arrive in Manchester because there is no way I could provide explanations for that, if it isn't me who answers the door.'

NEWTON: 'Right well I think that's it then right um yeah I mean don't forget you know that there's a charge you know that they can put on you is – us – a conspiracy to bloody –'

HOLMES: [interrupting] 'I am remembering that very carefully.'

NEWTON: ' – to murder right so now let's keep it quiet OK.'

HOLMES: 'Just fine and you may rely on that.'

The problem of Newton's job was never solved. Holmes had suggested he should go to Rhodesia, where General Peter Walls would be expecting him. Newton was handed an air ticket which he promptly exchanged for a cheaper one on a different airline. Before that he had paid some unsuccessful visits with his girl friend, Eleanor Rooney, to Holmes's house in Manchester. 'We didn't go inside but spent our time walking through the bushes. He didn't want to see me.'

Newton came back from Rhodesia, having failed to see General Walls. He closed his evidence, a touch of apparent resentment in his voice: 'I was welcomed again by the police.'

Newton's cross-examination was fierce, led off by Gareth Williams, Deakin's aggressive QC. Williams, who used every opportunity to emphasize his love of his home country of Wales, was by far the sharpest of the lawyers. He pushed the witnesses along, asking questions with quick-fire rapidity and dictating their answers firmly to the clerk Winder before darting back with the next question. Occasionally he over-reached himself, and Peter Taylor would interrupt from his seat three places along to point out that that was not precisely what the witness had said. Williams started off, in typical fashion, on Newton.

'Do you not find it difficult to distinguish between

fact and fantasy regarding this case?' 'Yes.' 'You have told a fair number of lies?' 'Yes.' 'Quite deliberately for your own purposes?' 'Yes.' 'The reasons were partly financial and partly to save your own skin?' 'Yes.'

Like Bessell, Newton had been given immunity by the Director of Public Prosecutions. And Williams wanted to underline the point. He picked up a sheet of paper and read the immunity out in full to the court. It gave him immunity from prosecution for conspiracy to murder Scott, for attempting to murder Scott, and for perjury at his last trial.

Williams had apparently scored a point straight away. From then on, the defence lawyers constantly referred to Newton as a man who had admitted he could not tell fact from fantasy. And they were determined to prove that he was a liar.

Williams took Newton through all the lies he had admitted telling. As well as lying on oath at his trial, he had produced false allegations that Norman Scott himself was a blackmailer with 'an enormous mass of circumstantial detail'. He had persuaded a Mrs Falkener to back up his story. Then Williams turned to his own concern: 'Did you agree to kill Norman Scott?'

'Yes,' asserted Newton, although he added he eventually changed his mind. The conspirators were supposed to have been introduced at the Showman's dinner in Blackpool. Was not Newton so drunk that he could not stand, was sick and got into a fight at the hotel? Newton did not remember the fight. Williams now made two suggestions on behalf of Deakin. Deakin had really told Newton someone was being blackmailed, a woman had already committed suicide and a young child was having its life threatened. Later he had told Newton the affair was not his problem, passing on the number in Manchester of David Holmes. No, said Newton, this was not right.

Chequebook journalism reared its head again. Newton had apparently broadcast on American TV that the *London Evening News* had a price on the heads of

Detective Chief Superintendent Michael Challes *(left)* and
Detective Superintendent David Greenough, of the Avon and
Somerset Constabulary, at Heathrow Airport after interviewing
Bessell in California

The prosecuting counsel at Minehead: Peter Taylor QC *(left)* and
John Bull

Rt Hon. Jeremy Thorpe MP. PC (with his wife, Marion)

John Le Mesurier

David Holmes

George Deakin

Norman Scott

Peter Bessell

Jack Hayward

Nadir Dinshaw

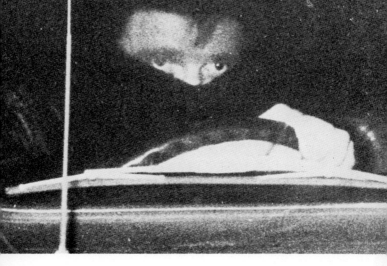

Far left: Rinka

Left: Andrew Gino Newton

Right: Sir David Napley, Thorpe's solicitor

Left: Newton (in balaclava) drives away from court

Right: Jeremy Thorpe MP at the Liberal Party Assembly in 1962

Pencourt: Barry Penrose (*right*) and Roger Courtiour

Minehead media. 'The eyes of the world' on the court-house

people, Williams said. There was £150,000 for Newton if he could implicate ex-Labour Prime Minister, Harold Wilson, in the murder conspiracy; £100,000 for Thorpe; and £65,000 for Holmes. Yes it was true, Newton said. Stuart Kuttner of the *News* had listed prices with £100,000 on Thorpe's head. But this did not mean the money was waiting for him. 'I think the *London Evening News* is also living in a fantasy world.'

'What position does Stuart Kuttner hold?' Newton answered: 'A dream-boat journalist.' The offer had been made before he set off for Rhodesia.

The following day at court, Tuesday 28 November, there was the usual chequebook journalism on a lesser scale as reporters handed over £5 and £10 notes to locals who had stood in the queue since early in the morning, enabling them to have a leisurely breakfast and still get a place in the public gallery.

That day also saw the first witness, Peter Bessell, leave England. Despite Thorpe's apparent loathing of him, as shown in the Hayward letters, Bessell said that as far as he was concerned 'I don't think our relationship has altered. At least I hope it hasn't.' He gave a last example of his art of understatement – 'but I am quite willing to accept that after what has transpired in the past week, Mr Thorpe may not feel quite the same'.

At court it was chequebook journalism again. Gareth Williams screwed Newton down to a precise list of the payments he had had. After close questioning they were finally agreed as: the *Evening News* – £3000; *Der Spiegel* – £4000; ABC – £2000; CBS – £500; the *Daily Express* – £600; Canadian Broadcasting – £500. He accepted that the total, including money he had spent from the pay-off, was about £12,000. He was still looking for a publisher for a book, from which he hoped for a return of about £50,000. He admitted that if any of the defendants were acquitted the libel laws would be a problem. Williams: 'Would you agree you have the clearest possible motive for perjuring yourself in this case?' 'I agree that is a possibility.'

Williams homed in. 'This case is your little pot of gold, isn't it?' Newton replied with an attempt at philosophy: 'Life is everything you have to lose.' Williams was not interested in philosophy. He dictated to Winder, after obtaining the answer from Newton: 'It is the only source of income that I have.' He followed it up: 'And you have resolved to milk it as hard as you can?' 'That is right.'

He admitted it was true he went to see Holmes in October 1977 at his house in Manchester in order deliberately to provoke a phone call and get extra evidence for his newspaper package. But it was not just for cash, he insisted. Newton rode over Williams's questioning – he wanted to tell the court about two attempts on his life. A torrent or words poured out which Winder tried to halt by holding up his hand like a policeman, a pained expression on his face as he tried to translate them fast enough on to the recording machine. Newton said somebody had tried to kill him in February 1976 in New York by knocking him down with a truck, and then running over him three times. This was just before his trial at Exeter, and he realized it would be 'very convenient' if he had not appeared, as 'sensitive matters' could not then be brought to public attention.

In July 1977, after he had come out of prison, a red Mini with two occupants had tried to scrape him along the wall near his mother's house. 'I can only assume this was either a warning to me to keep quiet or to do permanent harm to me.' He wanted to remind the court that, until this second attempt on his life, he had remained totally silent. Williams was not looking very impressed or interested in these stories.

Hadn't Newton told someone that BOSS (South African Intelligence) or British Intelligence had been involved in a break-in in his premises? Yes, Newton replied. And what about the pink roster sheets on which he had written down what Scott said? Were there names of prominent persons on the pink form? There were. Newton admitted he had tried to make money out of selling the pink documents. 'Nobody has a copy of the pink paper,' he said, definitely.

Williams swept his eyes along the lawyers either side of him. 'I think we ought to tell you we all have one here,' he said slowly and sarcastically. 'Have you ever had psychiatric treatment?' Newton came back quickly: 'No. But I am sure you will recommend me for some.' There was laughter.

Williams turned to a point directly concerning his client, Deakin – the meeting at Aust service station, on the M4. He suggested that Newton couldn't give an accurate date because it would then be checked. Where was the catalogue Deakin was supposed to have given him? 'I burnt that,' Newton replied. 'The truth is you never met Deakin at Aust.' 'We met all right.' He could not, on the other hand, remember the day of the week, where he had come from, or where he went afterwards.

Williams wanted to know whether his old student friend, Dave Miller, had been in the conspiracy to kill. 'Miller was aware,' Newton replied. 'He was a prime mover in putting me into contact with the people who wanted somebody eliminated.' And had he tried to kill Scott? 'I did not try to fire the gun at Norman Scott,' Newton emphasized. Williams pointed out that at his previous trial he said he was trying to fire a shot in Scott's general direction to frighten him but deliberately missed. This time he was saying the gun had jammed. But Newton stuck to his assertion: 'If I had tried to kill Norman Scott, I would have succeeded that night.'

'Are you a great fan of James Bond novels?' Williams asked. 'I prefer non-fiction books.' Wasn't it true he had fantasized having 'someone frightened' beyond all recognition, that he could not tell fact from fantasy and that he'd invented it, because he was being really very well paid? Newton denied it all and Williams sat down.

John Mathew, for Holmes, was also interested in the money Newton had got from the media – and particu-

larly the *London Evening News* (whose editor, Louis
Kirby, was another to issue a statement saying that he
was precluded from replying without infringing the possibilities of a fair trial). Newton was adamant about
Kuttner's role. 'He was bent on nailing Jeremy Thorpe
and David Holmes to a conspiracy to murder,' he said.
He might even sue' the *Evening News* for breach of
promise for a sum of around £60,000. He was paid
£3000 for merely allowing the paper to take a note of
part of the tape and allowing a voice comparison to be
made. Mathew brought up the journalists, Pencourt.
For once, he and Newton were in agreement. Mathew
produced an undated letter addressed 'Dear Mr
Holmes' and signed at the bottom with the initials
'A.N.'. The letter was supposedly sent from Preston,
where Newton was in prison, and asked Holmes to send
a card to Newton's mother's house saying: '"See you
soon, everything stands. Regards to Andy."' The letter
went on: '"Just sign it Davie. I'll quickly know everything is OK."'

'Penrose and Courtiour arranged for it to be sent
using your initials, didn't they?' Mathew asked. Newton
replied: 'I understand that is the case, and it was without my knowledge, co-operation or consent.'

Then came a macabre allegation. Had it ever been
Newton's plan to shoot Scott at the Royal Garden
Hotel, decapitate him and then take a photograph of
the corpse? 'Certainly not,' replied Newton sharply.
Mathew, at the far end of the lawyers' bench and staring straight ahead most of the time – only occasionally
turning to his witness – worried at the point. Eventually
Newton said: 'If it had been said, it could certainly just
have been a joke.' Nobody laughed.

Mathew went back to his major point. Newton
claimed to have had a number of meetings with Holmes
between November 1975 and February 1976, shortly
before his Exeter trial. He had also gone to Holmes's
house to provoke a telephone call in October 1977?
Yes, to get him on tape. But again it was not just for the

100

money. 'The reason was as a protection on my part in case anything happened to me. All the conspirators were put on tape so if a successful attempt on my life were made tapes would be made available to the press. David Holmes was missing on the insurance.'

What about the other six or seven meetings – could he give a date? No, Newton conceded.

Mathew challenged Newton unsuccessfully about his dramatic experience with a truck in America. Did he go to hospital? Yes he did, and could find out the name if required. And he also reported it to police. Mathew sat down and Newton briefly agreed with Le Mesurier's counsel that he had never encountered the Welshman before the St Brides Common pay-off. Sir David had no questions.

Then Taylor set out to bring Newton's evidence back on the Crown's rails. Newton had trouble again. 'Excuse me, do you and I get a chance to talk?' he asked. 'You must just answer the questions,' Taylor said stonily. There were no inducements from police, Newton agreed, other than that his statement would not be used against him. David Holmes had helped concoct his false story at the Exeter trial. And no – no one put a price on Deakin's head to him.

Newton's two days in the limelight were over. Attention had already shifted to the witness everyone had been waiting for. He had been hanging about waiting for Newton to finish, and would now have to come on the following morning. The TV news that night showed him tending his animals in his tumble-down Devon cottage. At last, Norman Scott, the man who claimed he went to bed with Jeremy Thorpe, was to have his say.

6

Norman Scott

Norman Scott is tall and holds himself stooped, with very short hair, slicked and parted. When he walked into court that morning in his quiet grey suit and dark tie with his open-air face, he had the manner of an over-grown public schoolboy. Only when Scott's voice rose in annoyance, as it was frequently to do in the days ahead, was it possible to see the complexity of his emotional make-up.

Thorpe, on his usual 'front bench' out of Scott's sight-line, stared fixedly at him in the witness box for a time, cupping a hand round his face. They had not met face to face for fifteen years. Thorpe's mother vanished from her usual seat beside Marion, and did not re-appear until Norman Scott left the precincts of the court. Interest had quickened elsewhere: tourists were pictured that morning rolling up their sleeping bags in the queue for public seats.

Of the witnesses so far, Bessell had given evidence of Thorpe's intention to plot murder; Hayward had testified about the means to finance the alleged conspiracy; and Newton had claimed to describe the actual method. Now Scott's role was to testify about motive. That he pestered Thorpe and claimed to be able to expose him, would, Sir David pointed out later, be enough of a motive – if Scott was likely to be believed. There was no denying, however, that what the press concentrated on was Scott's detailed and intimate description of a homosexual affair.

When the 21-year-old Norman Scott turned up at the House of Commons that day in 1961, he was in a bad state. He had just spent a month in a psychiatric clinic after a nervous breakdown and had a bandaged wrist; and he no longer worked at the Oxfordshire stables of 'the Hon. Van Der Breck der Vater'. 'His real name was Norman Vater, the son of a coal-face worker from Wolverhampton,' Scott dictated to the court. It was there that he had encountered Thorpe for the first time, when the MP told him Vater was a financial worry. 'If I had any problem of any sort, I was to get in contact with him.'

Scott was uncertain about the exact date when he arrived in London: 'I can remember the pink cherries were out as I drove over to Cherwell.' Thorpe told him not to worry. He was to go and collect Mrs Tish, his Jack Russell terrier, and come home with Thorpe. 'First of all we went to a flat in Dulwich. There were two friends of his there – a man I can remember as Tony and another man. We had a drink. He said he wanted them to look after me as he was going away the following day.' But he did not see them again.

Then came what Scott called 'the first lie'. Once at Stonewalls, Thorpe's mother's house in Oxted, he had to write a false name in the visitors' book. He was supposed to be 'Peter somebody, who lived in Colchester', one of the camera crew due to accompany Thorpe to Malta the next morning. 'When Mrs Thorpe went out of the room, I even had to ask him what county Colchester was in.' Taylor made him study the visitors' book, handed over by the defence. It said: '"November 8 1961. Norman Lianche-Josiffe, The Lodge."' Scott said the last part of the name was not in his writing or in the same pen. It looked as if there was something underneath it, although the address 'The Lodge' could be in his handwriting. Yet he had not lived there until much later, in 1971 in Dorset. 'It looks as if there's something underneath it . . . there's a small blot . . . I cannot see. Very faintly there's a beginning of some word.' (Josiffe was Scott's original name. Lianche was a 'frenchified' version of his mother's maiden name, Lynch, which he used to add.) There was another entry, which Scott recognized, for three days that Christmas.

Scott stayed the night. 'I went to the bedroom. I had to take sleeping pills and Jeremy came in with some water for me. He also bought a book in case I didn't fall asleep straight away – *Giovanni's Room* by James Baldwin. 'I discovered when I started to read it was a story of a relationship between two men. He said he thought I would like it.'

Taylor produced a copy; Sir David jumped to his feet and objected: it was a later impression of the book in Taylor's hand. This would not do. Taylor put the book down, but Scott went on: 'It describes, all the way through, how one man loves another man – in fact, it's a very beautiful story. . . .

'He came in an hour or so after he had left the first time. He was wearing pyjamas and a dressing gown. He just sat on the bed and talked to me – I had taken pills so I was quite woozy. He said: "You mustn't look so frightened, you mustn't look so worried: it's going to be all right. You've had a dreadful time, you look like a frightened rabbit." For me, it felt marvellous because I felt someone cared . . . I started to cry.

'He said: "You mustn't cry, you mustn't be unhappy," and he put his arms around me. Then he got into bed. He kissed me to start with and then went out to get a towel and a tube of some stuff. . . .' Scott broke off: 'It's really rather offensive to talk about it.' Taylor told him to continue.

'He put the towel underneath me and made love to me. He put this stuff on to his penis.' Was Scott active or passive? 'I was just biting the pillow. He was cutting me open with his penis.' Scott said he could not shout out because he did not want to offend or frighten Mrs Thorpe, whose room he thought was near by.

Scott did have a feeling towards men, although he had had a relationship with a girl at fifteen: 'I had homosexual relationships with other people prior to that occasion – but not the penetration.

'After the sex act, Mr Thorpe wiped himself off, got out of bed and went out of the room. About two hours later he came back and did the same thing. I just lay there on my bed and cried. There was nothing I could do, I was just stuck really. I thought I'd come somewhere to be protected. . . .

'He came in again at 7.30 a.m. and I thought he was going to do it again. I was very frightened. But he just didn't mention it. He asked me how I wanted my eggs done.'

Afterwards Thorpe told him he would pay the rent on a flat Scott found in Draycott Place, near Westminster; he would sort out his Insurance cards with Vater; and he could buy shoes on account from Thorpe's tailor, Gieves, in Old Bond Street. He got shoes, cellular underwear and, either then or later, two pairs of silk pyjamas. He also got two pale blue shirts from Thresher and Glenny.

'Thereafter he used to come in the evenings to my room, ostensibly just to see me – it was always the inevitable sex.' Scott went to Thorpe's mother's house, to the Reform Club, and to the House of Commons. Thorpe wanted him near by at Christmas in North Devon. He arranged for Scott to stay with the Colliers, and the four of them, with Thorpe's mother, Ursula, met for lunch once at the Broomhills Hotel in Barnstaple.

'He wanted to make love to me. He suggested we went upstairs . . . he suggested I go up and try on a shirt – that's what he said to the Colliers. They and Mrs Thorpe went for a walk around the garden.' Thorpe made love to him in the green-tiled bathroom of his hotel room. 'I stayed that night with him and he made love to me.' At the back of the court-room, Thorpe was rapidly making notes.

There were other nights with Thorpe, and two quarrels. 'We had a dreadful row when he was driving me over to the Colliers. I'm not trying to excuse myself. I just didn't want the sexual part of it – the friendship was nice. It always came down to the wretched sexual thing and I just hated it.

'He kissed me . . . I said I just wanted the whole thing to end. I began to cry: it was stupid of me. I said: "I must end it, I don't know how." He laughed at me. I said I thought he was absolutely rotten. It sounds ridiculous now but I said: "I'll show you up in public if you don't leave me alone." He laughed and said I sounded like a suburban person . . . "Anyway, one of my greatest friends is the Director of Public Prosecutions".'

The morning break intervened, and Thorpe shot straight out of the court-room through the side door and down the stairs, not pausing to speak to Marion as he went past the public benches. Ten minutes later he was back and seemed composed. He pointedly leaned across the press benches and said to Auberon Waugh, known to be writing a book on the affair: 'Well, how's the author?'

'Once it was Jeremy who thought he'd like to end it all,' Scott went on, 'because it was getting too difficult. He drove a Sunbeam Rapier with a very long bonnet and he really frightened me. I begged him to slow down. He said it wouldn't matter if we did crash, it would be a way out of the situation.' On that occasion [which he did not specify exactly] when they arrived at their destination, the Colliers' house, Scott was highly upset and ill, he said. He spoke to Mary Collier.

Now the court reached the 'Bunnies' letter, which had already been published in the newspapers. Taylor kept one name out as he read it and Scott said '1961' was a mistake for 1962:

'February 13, 1961
'House of Commons

'My dear Norman,
    'Since my letters normally go to the House, yours arrived
all by itself at my breakfast table at the Reform, and gave me
tremendous pleasure.
    'I cannot tell you just how happy I am to feel that you are
really settling down, and feeling life has something to offer.
    'This is really wonderful and you can always feel that what-
ever happens, Jimmy and Mary and I are right behind you.
The next thing is to solve your financial problem and this
James Walters and I are on to. The really important point is
that you are now a member of a *family*, doing a useful job of
work – with Tish – which you enjoy. Hooray! Faced with all
that, no more bloody clinics.
    'I think you can now take the [———————— ——————————]
incident as over and done with. Enclosed another ltr!! I suggest you keep them all – just in case – but will you send back
the photo? Thank the guy but say you are fixed up. In haste.

'Bunnies *can* (and *will*) go to France.
    'Yours affectionately,
    'Jeremy
    'I miss you.'

    'Bunnies' was his 'frightened rabbit' pet name, Scott
said. The hand-written 'ltr' looked like 'lvr', and Scott
had assumed it meant 'lover'. It was a joke between
them because Thorpe had put an advertisement in
Country Life for Scott: 'We laughed about it because so
many of the replies were from homosexuals, who just
wanted some young man to go and live with them.'
Taylor now produced the text *Country Life* sent back to
Thorpe for confirmation: 'Ex-public-schoolboy ...
desires live with family. Pocket money only.' It was
Scott's ultimate dream to do a dressage course in
France, he said. James Walters was the lawyer sorting
out the Vater problem and the 'incident' was over a
sheepskin coat Scott was supposed to have stolen. A
policeman arrived at Thorpe's office in Bridge Street to
see Scott about it: 'When the policeman arrived, the

door was locked and Jeremy Thorpe was making love to me.'

There was another brief note that autumn from the House of Commons, on 30 September. Thorpe was 'terribly sad to hear about poor little Mrs Tish'. Scott had become depressed again: Mrs Tish had been destroyed after it killed all the ducks at the home of a Dr Lister at Porlock Weir on the north Devon coast. Scott had been staying there and working at stables in Minehead (half a mile from the court-room). He had got in touch with Jeremy to ask him for a photo of him holding his dog, Tish.

Back at the Draycott Place flat, and still 'pretty suicidal', Scott said he started seeing a lot of Thorpe again, mostly in the evenings. In desperation he decided to kill both himself and Thorpe, and moved out to the Easton Hotel in Victoria: 'I was very unhappy.' He told a mutual woman friend about things: he was also astonished to discover the hotel receptionist was none other than Mary Collier. Two policemen rapidly collected Scott from the hotel and he made a statement to officers Smith and Huntley (later to lead the Bomb Squad) at the police station, giving them the two letters quoted 'and others'. The police had eventually given him the two letters quoted back but maintained there were no other letters to return to him.

That Christmas, Norman Scott spent with his mother. He gave more details of sex with Thorpe: 'What we used to do, I would meet him at the House in the evenings, and he would say that I could spend ten minutes with him. We'd just drive down to Battersea Bridge . . . we'd just masturbate in the car. At Marsham Court [Thorpe's own flat] he would make love to me and then . . . ask me to get out. He kept a small collapsible bed in the wardrobe. I'd have to sleep on that.'

A job in Switzerland looking after horses was advertised in *Horse and Hound*. Scott wanted to get away and, he said, Thorpe paid for the journey and arranged a passport, signing the photos. Scott was back after one day there, having lost his luggage on the train, deciding the place was 'really ghastly' and turning up at Marsham Court.

The lost luggage actually contained all Thorpe's letters to Scott, he told him – 'he had written about fifty letters to me'. Homosexuality was an imprisonable offence at the time, Scott explained: 'He was not very pleased with me at all.'

Scott did not stay with Thorpe. 'It was just that physical thing again,' he said. He went off to Belfast, and had a homosexual affair there. He also injured himself falling off a horse. 'I used to ring up Jeremy and say: "Please can you sort out my Insurance cards?"' Thorpe was supposed to have taken over the whole problem left by Vater. Also Scott's luggage was still missing. Thorpe kept promising things would be sorted out, and Scott, who had confided in the priest, Father Sweetman, finally sat down and wrote the Dublin letter to Mrs Ursula Thorpe. The letter, already read out to Peter Bessell, was handed over to Scott. 'I haven't read it for years,' he remarked, sitting down and going through it. Two events had been transposed, said Scott: 'I was in a very emotional state and sedated . . . things were getting into a dreadful jumble.' Otherwise it was correct.

After Scott had sent off the letter, Peter Bessell suddenly arrived in Dublin. According to Scott, he began aggressively by saying he had an extradition order signed by Frank Soskice, the Home Secretary, to take him back to England on a charge of blackmail. Scott had taken the wind out of his sails by saying: '"That's absolutely marvellous. I want to go back to England. I haven't been blackmailing anybody: I just want to get things sorted out."' Scott explained his finances were bad because of the Insurance card. Bessell said he really did believe him and promised to recover his luggage, although he lectured him that Mrs Thorpe had known nothing of the relationship and it was wrong of Scott to have written: '"I mustn't ever write to her again," he told me.'

When the luggage finally arrived at Dublin airport, battered and broken, the Thorpe letters were missing and so were some shirts with Marsham Court laundry marks on them.

Bessell had also offered to try and help him get work in America. Scott wrote to him subsequently. Sir David produced some of the letters. Why did the handwriting vary so much? 'My writing changes all the time – if I was feeling extrovert, it would perhaps be larger than if I was worried.' He was getting a little modelling work, having changed his name to Scott ('people kept thinking my name was Joe Sieff'). Bessell, having talked to Thorpe, agreed that until his final departure, he would pay money every week in lieu of 'National Insurance benefit'.

It was lunch-time. Up the road at the Kildare Motor Lodge, where the reporters gathered for a quick lunch, the conversation was distinctly more animated than usual.

If the morning had been about sex, the afternoon was very definitely about violence. The evidence also went at a much faster pace. The lawyers had met over the break and decided that as Scott was less than a quarter of the way through his evidence, he could be asked 'leading questions'. Taylor took Scott rapidly through the £75 given to him by Bessell to set up as a model and his brief marriage to Susan Myers from May 1969 to early 1971 when it broke up. The couple had had one son, Diggory Benjamin Scott. Bessell had suggested Scott go on a world cruise, but he did not want to: he went instead to live in an old mill house in north Wales, where things went well until Ross, the divorce solicitor engaged for him by Bessell, had given Scott the impression he was not acting in his best interest. 'I felt it was the beginning of a very large cover-up,' he said, '. . . I tried once again to kill myself.' Scott had taken sleeping pills. He had recovered and met Mrs Parry-Jones, a widow, with whom he lived.

In May 1971 the two had gone together to the House

of Commons and seen David Steel, now Leader of the Liberal Party, Emlyn Hooson, and Lord Byers. They talked to them and showed them Scott's file of documents. A few days later on 10 June, he went to Southwark police station and made a statement. Shortly after, Mrs Parry-Jones killed herself, and Scott's divorce went through undefended at Boston County Court in Lincolnshire. [Later in the hearing Sir David Napley referred to a public outburst made by Scott at the inquest about his alleged relationship with Thorpe.]

By 1973 Scott had moved to South Molton, in Thorpe's constituency. 'I did not go there with that intention,' he said, to explain it had not been malicious. His health was bad and he consulted Dr Ronald Gleadle, who, Scott said, used to write 'nervous anxiety' on his surgery pad when he saw him. Scott said he visited London and went to a party.

Scott broke off in his evidence and asked for some water. Clearly finding it difficult to cope with the pace of events as Taylor took him through them, he said: 'My mind has gone completely blank.' He remembered and carried on. He had met Gordon Winter, a South African journalist, and told him his story. Winter had photocopied all the documents in what he called 'the Bessell file'.

Taylor slowed when he came to the crucial night of 27 February 1974, the day before the General Election. Scott explained he took his sleeping pills and went to bed. Abouth 8.45 p.m. Dr Gleadle came in and asked where the Bessell file was. Scott asked what he was doing, and Gleadle said he would explain it all later. He had to give to to somebody. 'His words were: "The sky's the limit."'

The next day Gleadle had paid a total of £2500 into two bank accounts which he had opened for Scott, but refused to say where it had come from.

Scott had got worried that he had now lost any real evidence and contacted Winter to try to get the photostats. He said he was drinking heavily and was very nervous.

Nearly a year later, on 4 February 1975, he had gone to the Imperial Hotel, Barnstaple to meet a 'Mr Steiner' who had rung him saying he was from *Der Spiegel*, the German news magazine. He had taken with him all his documents, along with a modelling catalogue he was featured in, as 'Steiner' had requested. Two men arrived and sat in the lounge where Scott was waiting. He was called to take a telephone call and, he said, 'I stupidly left my documents in the sitting room.' The call was from 'Steiner' who said he had to go back to London because Margaret Thatcher had been made Leader of the Opposition. When he returned, the men, and the documents, had gone. Scott had described one of the men as '"rather short and strong"' and the other as having '"short-cropped hair".'

Scott also recalled being telephoned by a man with a rather rough-sounding voice calling himself '"Ian Wright"' and saying he was from a company called Pinserio. The man offered him a modelling job at a fee of £400 a day and asked him to come to London to discuss it. 'I said it was absolutely ludicrous. I thought the whole thing was just some crank.' He refused to go. He also refused to go to see the supposed journalist 'Masterson' (Newton, in his evidence, said the name used was 'Matheson') telling him plaintively that it would not be too difficult for him to come and see him in Barnstaple, where he was then living.

Taylor then took Scott on to his first meetings with the man he knew as 'Keene', who was really Newton. 'Keene' had asked him to go to a lay-by where a woman was waiting for him. But Scott refused. 'He got quite annoyed. He said: "I wish you'd fucking well come with me."' Instead they went to a pub. 'I showed him the evidence and talked about what had happened. He made notes on pink paper.' Keene suggested all he had to do was to pass the documents to the lawyer Michael Barnes, and sign something to say everything he had ever said was a complete lie. In return he would be given a great deal of money. Scott refused.

'Keene' rang him on 23 October. 'The caller said: "Hullo, it is Andy." I said: "I don't know anybody called Andy." He said: "No, no, no, oh no, it's Peter."' 'Keene' said Scott was in great danger and he was coming down to protect him. They arranged to meet the next day. Scott by that stage had a great dane, Rinka, who friends had given him a week before. He took the dog to the meeting. 'Keene' was upset and said: '"I don't want that bloody dog in the car."' But Scott refused to go without her and they set off from Combe Martin along the coast road to Porlock, with Scott clutching 'Keene's' book on Scientology and briefcase on his lap, and Rinka taking up most of the back of the Ford Escort. 'Keene' told him he was a special investigator and had to see somebody in Porlock who he was thinking of employing. Scott was left at the Castle Hotel and thought 'Keene' had forgotten him. He went out to find transport and found 'Keene' sitting in the car across the road. They set off up the steep Porlock hill. The car started swaying and veering over the road. Scott offered to drive and 'Keene' (Newton's alias) pulled on to a remote spot on the top of the moors. Scott got out and told Newton to just move over so that Rinka would not jump out. 'She would have made the car all wet because it was pouring with rain,' he said. 'I ran round the front of the car. As I came round through the lights his door was already open and a light was showing. He was standing there. Rinka came bounding to meet me. She thought we were going for a walk. She was jumping around outside the car. I said: "I am so sorry. I meant just move over."'

'He said: "Oh no, this is it," and shot her. I did not realize he had shot her then. She just crumpled down in front of me.'

By this time everyone in court could see the tears in Scott's eyes, and he apologized in a broken voice when Taylor asked if he had heard anything. 'It was so windy.

. . . It's all so vague.' He tried to recover himself. 'I said: "I don't know why you have included her."' Scott stopped and broke down again. 'I can't think . . . I am sorry,' he said, wiping tears from his cheeks. 'I just knelt down to shake her. I couldn't really work out what had happened. I said: "You can't involve a dog, you can't involve an animal."'

Scott raised his right arm in the dock to indicate how he had felt 'this thing' behind him. 'The next thing I was aware of was him standing in the headlights of the car. He said: "It's your turn now." I was still going down to Rinka. I wasn't aware, really aware, of what he was meaning when he said that . . . I turned to look for him and he was in the car headlights. My arms were round Rinka.' Scott paused and sniffed audibly. 'He was just shaking whatever he had in his hand.' Scott made a flapping motion with his right hand extended, moving it up and down. 'He was screaming – it was horrid – saying: "Oh Fuck it! Fuck it! Fuck it!"'

'I suddenly realized what was happening. I realized he was going to kill me. He levelled the gun at me. I still didn't realize it was a gun. I suddenly came to life and I began to run – maybe three to four strides. Then I realized I was running into the lights on the horizon, which was Wales, and was a target. I thought if I was going to die I might as well go back to Rinka so I went back.

'He levelled this thing at me again, shouted: "Oh fuck it! – I'll get you," slewed the car over, bounced it off the rise we were on, and drove back towards Porlock.'

Scott had stayed with Rinka. 'I was trying to give her the kiss of life. I was crying and screaming for her and screaming at God. I saw headlights coming over the moor and I ran out and flagged the car down. I said: "Oh please. He's shot my dog. He tried to shoot me."'

Taylor inturrupted gently and asked if he could remember saying anything else. Scott replied: 'I know I did say: "It's all because of Jeremy Thorpe."'

Gareth Williams, for Deakin, and John Mathew, for Holmes, had only brief cross-examinations.

Sir David Napley stood up. He would be starting his cross-examination the next morning – Wednesday. He warned: 'It will take a considerable time.'

7

Scott cross-examined

Scott was to be in the witness box for a day and a half before Sir David finished with him. He was clearly tense as he walked into court, ignoring Thorpe and taking up his position in the witness box with his hands resting lightly on the top of the wooden panelling. He wore a dark brown double-breasted suit, but the cut of it and his small check short and woollen tie again had the slightly dated look that characterized his clothing.

Sir David started gently: 'It wouldn't be surprising if you were a little worried or apprehensive this morning?' Scott replied firmly: 'I am not at all worried or apprehensive.' 'It is not my intention or desire to be in any way unkind to you,' Sir David added, shuffling the papers in front of him. His voice quickened. Hadn't Scott had a copy of *The Pencourt File* on his lap when he drove to the court the previous day? 'No,' said Scott, offended. 'It was a copy of Anglo-Saxon poetry.'

This first skirmish over, Sir David had Scott establish that he had previously told people he was a minor when the relationship with Thorpe started. Scott blamed the error on the wrongly dated 'Bunnies' letter and said it didn't matter because homosexuality itself was 'an imprisonable offence at that time' anyhow.

Sir David clearly wanted to paint a picture of what sort of man Scott was, and took him slowly through his background – primary school in Bexleyheath, and a secondary modern. As a juvenile he had been sent away under a Fit Person Order as in need of care and protection. He was never sure who his father was and he

116

agreed he had written to Bessell that his mother had sent him away so she could continue her affairs.

The questioning was clearly agitating Scott, and he made the first of several outbursts in a stormily emotional day. Why did his mother have to be discussed in court? 'Why are you doing it? I would like to know.' Sir David said he was sorry, but he had to. He forged on. 'That's really been the problem. You had a deprived childhood. You have spent the rest of your life looking for love and affection.' Scott replied: 'I did, but when I found how bad it was when I was so let down by your client, I decided I must just get on with things in my own way and things would evolve. I don't think my life is tragic any more.'

Had he found Thorpe kind, sympathetic and understanding? 'Yes. I thought he was a wonderful person then – before I realized what he was like.' Wasn't it right to say Scott alternated between periods of frustration and self-pity, and periods of anger? Scott's reply, again, was that times had changed. 'Right. But I don't have this "self-pity thing" any more because I think, purely in a philosophical way, these things are meant to happen. The truth will come out and that will be that.'

Sir David replied by quoting him two lines by William Congreve:

'"Heav'n has no rage, like love to hatred turn'd
Nor Hell a fury, like a woman scorn'd"

– does not that describe your position, Mr Scott?' Scott replied tartly: 'I am not a woman.' He added: 'I think anybody would be angry, whether a man or a woman, at the way I have been treated –' his voice rose '– and continue to be treated, Sir David.'

Sir David took him through allegations made by former associates or employers – stealing a handbag; saying his father was alternatively in North America, killed in an air crash, or working in the British Embassy in Paris and a Frenchman; and stealing a £20 deposit on a horse. Van der Vater had described him as 'an abso-

117

lute scoundrel and a horse thief'. Scott replied: 'Van der Vater was an undischarged bankrupt. I would like to return that, and turn it totally round on Mr Van der Vater.'

After the generalities Sir David now came to details of fact.

Was it right to say on the night he alleged the relationship wih Thorpe started he had first been driven to a house in Dulwich? Taylor, for the Crown, intervened at this apparently sensitive point with a warning about naming names. Scott said it was a homosexual party. 'These two men were drinking and expecting some more people.' That night Thorpe brought him *Giovanni's Room*. He was reading it when Thorpe came in an hour later.

'Are you a truthful person?' Sir David asked. 'I have told many many lies in the past but I am truthful now. I have got to be because this is a very important thing.' Sir David turned to his 1962 police statement. Scott admitted he had not told the truth in that, but said it was because he was afraid of going to prison. 'I was afraid of saying in this statement he had actually physically penetrated me.' Sir David persisted. The 1962 statement said: '"I retired about twenty minutes after I had arrived."' Scott said that was not correct. In fact he had had dinner. Thorpe and his mother were talking separately, and she was showing him the newspaper clippings about Thorpe she cut out each day. 'I felt I was in the way and I was slightly out of my class,' he said.

Sir David looked up interestedly. 'Why do you say that?' Scott replied: 'I don't think I am very good class.' He paused. 'Is there such a thing any more? Certainly I do not think Sir David Napley's client is a good class of person,' he added petulantly. Losing his composure again, he burst out: 'You're saying this because you are trying to rile me. I am not here on trial. I am here because of that man who tried to destroy me over a period of years and I will not be destroyed.' Clearly upset, he stopped shouting and said penitently: 'I am sorry, Sir David. I am not trying to be rude.' 'Let me assure you I'm not trying to rile you. I am not trying to be rude either,' the lawyer rejoined. 'I am just doing a job.'

He asked him again what had happened that night. The 1962 statement said that Thorpe had come in, sat on the bed, and after talking for some time '"kissed me"'. 'He had a cloth with him and some Vaseline.' Sir David said that Scott had said in court yesterday Thorpe had left him for an hour and he had read parts of the book. But his police statement said it happened '"at once"'. Scott said that was not true. 'I was very very afraid of the police at that time. . . . I was afraid to describe it all. Words wouldn't come.' In his statement he had said: '"I'm almost certain his penis did not go into my anus."' Sir David said Scott had had homosexual experience before then, and would have had no difficulty in describing it in the 1962 statement. Scott replied: 'I had never had a complete physical relationship: the whole thing which happened with Thorpe.'

He agreed he was 'woozy'. But he added: 'I think anybody that sort of thing happened to would wake up pretty quickly. I had not had that complete experience before.' He admitted he had said nothing in the statement about two homosexual acts that night. 'It was because I was frightened.'

Sir David wanted something explaining. Scott had said he had had a 'frightful experience which sickened and disgusted him'. So why hadn't he got away from Thorpe? 'He came in the following morning and was so gentle and nice to me again. He asked what I wanted for breakfast. . . . You seem to forget I was very under these drugs. I was not really able to sort my life out.'

Sir David persisted in his worrying at detail. The next morning Scott had said they picked up Thorpe's secretary, Miss Jennifer King, and she drove. If she and her father both said no such thing happened, and had diaries, would they be mistaken? 'Absolutely,' said

Scott firmly. 'Of course Miss King is going to look after Mr Thorpe. She has loyalties to him.' Sir David did one of his swivelling motions to stare at the press bench behind him. He picked at more discrepancies, this time in the 1971 police statement. Scott gave the general reply which he repeated throughout his evidence: 'The dates may be wrong but things that happened happened.' And he said: 'What happened the night before had been horrendous but I felt about the night, as I thought about it, perhaps it was all I deserved. . . . I thought I was in love with Mr Thorpe.'

Sir David: 'You did not think he was in love with you?' Scott: 'I don't think Jeremy Thorpe is capable of loving anything except his power.' The court went very quiet, and Scott added after a few moments: 'I don't mean that in a vindictive way,' his eyes darting sideways towards Thorpe, sitting on the front bench. Sir David's next remarks were clearly deeply wounding. 'This fits in with your search for love and affection . . . the other thing you have now turned to is animals.' Scott shouted back: 'I have a daughter and a very beautiful girl friend who is not living with me at the moment because of this grotesque situation. I have a great love for animals but a much greater love for my daughter.' (Scott has a two year old daughter, Brionie, by his girl friend Hilary Arthur.) Sir David tried to interrupt him, but Scott had clearly had enough. Waving his arms about, he shouted again: 'I don't think I can take much more of this cross-examination, Sir David. There is one way of proving there was a relationship. I don't like to say it but I should like one prosecution counsel to have a witness and you to have a witness to take Mr Thorpe to another room and I will tell you something about him which I could not know if I had not slept with him. This is ridiculous. I can't keep going on and on. There is just a truthful way of getting this whole thing finished.' Winder, the clerk, looked despairing, unable to keep up with the torrent of words.

Thorpe turned his head to see how his wife Marion

was bearing up. She was blinking rapidly. Sir David tried to bring the tone down. He could not ask Scott about this unless he knew what it was. Scott replied more calmly: 'Of course; I know. I would not tell you until you have seen him.'

Sir David tried to go back to detail, and what Scott had told the Colliers. Scott replied he had 'recounted the substance' to Mary Collier, and later to her husband, Jimmy. The questioning did not last long. The court would see for itself what Mr Collier had to say, Scott retorted, shouting again in an exasperated fashion: 'I think it is too stupid. I don't really care what anybody says about it. I had a relationship. I am the person who is being destroyed still because of it. It is only myself and God after all. I wouldn't like to be Mr Thorpe going to see Him at some stage.' Sir David ignored it and ploughed on. Scott denied he had told 'Caroline' in 1962 that he was going to kill Thorpe and himself so as to bring pressure on him. 'I was upset so much and I just felt it was so awful. It was the first realization this whole thing was involving other people.'

The morning ended on a light note. Sir David was clearly shocked at the replies to the advertisement in *Country Life*. 'A reputable magazine,' he said with a pained expression. Scott was quite blunt: 'They were all from poofs or seemed to be.'

That afternoon, Scott's dramatic claim he could prove he had slept with Thorpe ended in bathos. Sir David prised out of him: 'Mr Thorpe, without his clothes, under one arm has something like warts or nodules. They are also somewhere else – I am not sure. I am not sure which arm.' He added rather hopelessly: 'Also his spinal column doesn't go straight, it sort of curves.' He gestured with his hands as John Le Mesurier, hitherto apparently uninterested in the proceedings, threw back his head with laughter. 'Ho! Ho! Ho!' he roared. Marion Thorpe smiled. Sir David's head swivelled towards the press, with an air of great disdain: 'I don't propose to have a medical examination under these circumstances.' Scott: 'I couldn't have seen them except without his clothes.'

Sir David and Scott now fell to quarrelling over what constituted 'making love'. Scott had told police in 1962, of the Bridge Street incident: '"He tried to kiss me, tried to get hold of my penis . . . there was a knock at the door."' Sir David: 'You make no distinction between having sex, and someone kissing a person and trying to get hold of his penis? . . . You said yesterday: "The door was locked . . . and Jeremy Thorpe was making love to me."' Scott said impatiently: 'He was making advances to me . . . does it really matter?' His [Scott's] flies had been undone.

Sir David raised a new matter. Hadn't Scott told Thorpe his father had died in an air crash, a story which had led to Thorpe engaging the lawyer, Walters, to see if it would be possible for Scott to claim compensation for the accident? It was not him who had been pretending, Scott replied. It was Thorpe who had made the whole story up, he explained, compressing his lips. 'He had decided to introduce me as this *orphan*.' Thorpe had once told the story to Lord Reith at the Reform Club. 'I wasn't of sufficient breeding,' Scott added.

Sir David said levelly: 'If that's your explanation. . . .' But didn't Scott go around pretending to be called 'The Honourable'? Scott came back sharply: 'Mr Van der Vater seemed to have achieved a great deal calling himself *'The Honourable'*. . . . Mr Thorpe held him in high esteem.' The lies to people he came in contact with were because he could not talk about Thorpe and homosexuality: 'There is nobody in the first twenty-five or thirty years of my life who doesn't think I am one of the most dreadful people ever, because of this situation, this lying about homosexuality and the relationship.' Had he told people that his wife and daughter had died in a car crash? 'I have told the most amazing lies, it's true.'

'To win sympathy?' 'To be able to eat!' Had he not imposed himself on a couple, the Weights? They said

122

so. The wife fancied him, Scott replied, and as for the husband: 'He's a cuckolded man. Of course he is going to bloody say it!'

Sir David now did something in tune with much of the hearing. A good deal of evidence was never read out in full, and both Crown and defence were obviously anxious to keep names out of the headlines if they could help it. Newton's sheets of pink paper, with names Scott had talked about, were never read out in court. And Scott himself at one point let slip: 'I know I am not supposed to mention names.' Now Napley gravely handed over a sheet of paper. There were 'two well-known names' on it. Didn't he tell Mrs Weight he had had homosexual relations with them?

Scott denied it. 'There's a slight difference in the sexuality of the two men anyway. . . . One is an obvious homosexual and one isn't.'

Father Sweetman, the Irish priest, had actually written a letter to Thorpe, Sir David now disclosed. It described Scott as: '"A thoroughly unreliable, unscrupulous and deceitful person."' Yes, he knew about the letter, Scott said. Some journalist had told him that Sweetman had been visited. 'He felt I was a very wicked person to be doing this to Jeremy Thorpe. . . . He was only doing what any good common God-fearing man would do. He was being honest as he saw it. . . . I had to tell dreadful lies to him.'

Having attacked Scott's honesty, Sir David now started to develop his own scenario. Scott had been in a 'frightful state', threatening suicide once more and in desperate need of help. Thorpe had been worried Scott would be lonely over Christmas when he met him. Scott asserted he had other friends to turn to such as Caroline Barrington-Ward. (A letter arrived at the *Guardian* the following day from Mrs Caroline Roberts, *née* Barrington-Ward, of Tring, Herts., asking them to point out she was not the woman referred to. The paper did.)

Then Scott started shouting at the top of his voice

across the court-room: 'Mr Thorpe was concerned about one thing – to keep on screwing me! Let's stop this pussyfooting, Sir David!' Sir David was not diverted. 'I am putting it to you when he said he was worried you would be lonely after Christmas, Mr Thorpe was fearful having regard to your condition.' Scott said wearily: 'No, not at all.'

Later he explained he had given a copy of everything to do with him and Thorpe to any reporter who had asked for it, including Pencourt. 'I was sick of the cover-up . . . you, Sir David, were part of the cover-up and you know well why!'

Sir David turned again to the involved affair of the Swiss luggage. Scott claimed two shirts were missing as well as a block of House of Commons notepaper when it finally got to Dublin. What had been removed 'meant there was nothing there to relate my life with Jeremy Thorpe', he explained.

What about the other letter – the Dublin letter to Mrs Ursula Thorpe, Thorpe's mother? Why had he written it? Scott had written to Bessell that he thought Mrs Thorpe knew of the affair. Why? 'Because every mother knows about her children,' said Scott haltingly. 'In retrospect do you think it was a pretty horrible thing to do?' Scott agreed, but he added: 'It was a desperate remedy.' And he finally gave an explanation for writing to Mrs Thorpe. 'I wanted to explain to her what it was all about. I was afraid her son would be blackmailed if anybody found the letters.' He added bitterly: 'Contrary to what everybody seems to think of me, Norman Scott the blackmailer.' And he had another dig at Van der Vater when Sir David raised his name. He had been a friend until he behaved so badly. And furthermore, Scott indignantly alleged, he had stung his pocket. 'Van der Vater borrowed money for a bogus funeral when it was really to go down to see Jeremy Thorpe at the House of Commons.'

Sir David decided to round off the day by cataloguing a few of Scott's stories in the past. The most outrageous was that Scott had allegedly said in Ireland he was the illegitimate son of a peer and was waiting to go into hospital for a leucotomy operation.

The day's – and that week's – proceedings fizzled out in a string of minor questions, and Sir David reserved major matters for the following Monday.

The court finished a day early at the end of the second week. The next day, Friday, had been set aside for more mundane and normal local matters. There was one 'found drunk', and 'goods to the value of 34½p' stolen from the local supermarket, with a string of minor motoring offences that had piled up over the last fortnight. Only one of the London evening papers stayed, to do an item for its diary.

The next Monday morning all the reporters were back, pencils sharpened. Scott, in a dark charcoal-grey suit, tensed his jaw as Sir David rose for more questioning. The solicitor wasted no time. 'Do you assert you had a homosexual relationship with Mr Thorpe?' 'Yes I do.' When he was a bachelor? 'Yes.' When Scott was a fully grown man? 'Yes.' Something over thirteen years ago? 'Yes.' He talked about a cover-up? 'Yes.'

Sir David slowed. He said measuredly: 'Of what, Mr Scott?' 'A cover-up which has evolved because of the relationship.' Sir David adopted a puzzled air – 'Explain it to me.' 'Because of the relationship and because Mr Thorpe had taken over my Insurance cards,' said Scott irritably. Then, as Sir David persisted, he said: 'It's a matter really just for myself and Mr Thorpe's moral conscience. I did not want this to evolve in this way.' His voice dropped and he muttered: 'It's a waste of public money.'

Scott agreed: 'It was a rather sordid affair,' and Sir David homed in on two of his main themes that morning – the Insurance cards and the 'cover-up'. Scott explained. 'Thorpe through his inherent meanness did not pay stamps for the Insurance card.' When he asked for it back Thorpe could not give it because it would have been an admission of the relationship. Sir David appeared incredulous. Was he seriously saying this was a reason for all this? 'I don't mind who or what Mr Thorpe is,' Scott said in an irritated fashion. 'What he did was take on a responsibility he didn't follow through to pay the Insurance card.' The moral responsibility of sleeping with Scott and the Insurance cards did link. 'It's a one-off situation but the two do link. I'm sorry.'

Taylor drummed his hands on the table. Scott was clearly becoming agitated. He clenched his hands and looked down at this feet. Sir David put on his incredulous voice again. 'Are you saying we are here today because you did not have an Insurance card paid up?' 'It was the only reason I talked about Jeremy Thorpe and myself,' Scott replied. 'Indeed,' he added, nodding his head in emphasis.

'Does this strike you as being rational?' Scott replied angrily that it did not matter. 'Things have evolved out of the relationship which have been incredibly irrational but I have been steadfast in my resolve to have what is my right – and I will continue.'

Sir David picked up a letter dated 27 April 1962. Addressed to Scott from the Social Security Office, it said the information had enabled them to confirm his National Insurance number was 7115100. It enclosed a National Insurance card valid until 2 September 1962. Sir David said this showed he had a card then and knew his number. 'I can't remember what was going on.' Scott tried to explain: when you didn't have a card fully paid up you could not get sickness benefit. 'You have to live off the charity and kindness of others.'

Sir David pointed out David Ennals had waived all Scott's contributions after eleven years. Scott retorted: 'I would go straight to David Ennals and ask why he waived the contributions for eleven years. Why should I have this privilege? I think it is incredibly corrupt, and a part of the cover-up. No person should be allowed to have anything waived in this way because of the misdemeanours of a fellow MP.' [Ennals later issued a statement saying he could not comment until after the trial.]

But Bessell had paid him the equivalent of unemployment benefit with the retainers? Scott said they had only been £5 a week. He was living at his mother's home. 'She is not a wealthy woman,' he said bitterly. 'I would not have brought your client in if I had not had any money. I don't do it for fun.' 'Really,' said Sir David. 'Then you do it for money?' Scott got cross as he tried to get his point across. He was looking for someone to stamp his card. Who? 'The Right Honourable John Jeremy Thorpe because he took on the responsibility, of course. We will be going around in circles for another three days, I can see that.' He made dismissive, puffing noises. 'Unlike you, Sir David, I will have to think about pensions and things like that.

'For goodness' sake. Thorpe would not *return* the card. . . .' He laughed slightly in exasperation. 'I *do* have other things to do than think about this case nowadays.' 'Do you?' said Sir David quickly. 'Yes, I am very busy all day every day.'

Sir David returned to the letters Scott had given the police in December 1962 and never had back. Were the police lying? 'No,' said Scott, 'They were covering something up.' 'They took letters from Jeremy to me but also to the man before that, Van der Vater, Thorpe's lover before me. Do you really want to go into this?' Circuitously, Sir David got instead to Scott's failed marriage. Scott claimed that his marriage would never have broken up if it had not been for money difficulties, which he blamed on not having a card. Every time he walked into an Insurance office they wanted to know the name of his previous employer. His emotion burst out again. 'You seem to have the idea I walked about Trafalgar Square shouting out: "I've slept with Jeremy Thorpe."' Scott calmed himself and asked for a glass of water. He cleared his throat. Sir David, more gently, prised out of him that his wife could not stand his relationships with another man, a Mr Conway

Wilson-Young, with whom Scott had lived around that time.

Scott was clearly nettled at the line of questioning. 'I would like to get this point over because you are trying to evade it,' he started shouting. 'I'm not here because of this homosexuality. I am here because somebody tried to kill me.'

Sir David came right back. 'You are here because you failed to stamp your National Insurance card.' 'I am here because of your client and my relationship. The Insurance card came after.'

What about his relationship with Mrs Parry-Jones? He was 31 at the time, she was 52. Scott said they had gone to see Mr Hooson at the Commons, not to get financial help but to sort out the Insurance cards. He agreed quietly she had committed suicide. 'I am sure this whole situation killed Gwen Parry-Jones no matter what anybody says. Ordinary people cannot believe corruption exists in the House of Commons.'

He added angrily: 'I did happen to love her, you know.'

'Do you have that lady's death on your conscience?' – 'Yes I do, and so does Mr Thorpe in a roundabout way. If he had paid the bloody cards none of this would have happened.' He added, almost to himself: 'Bloody cards,' and then looked up and said: 'I'm sorry.' Sir David asked if suicide was part of Scott's normal pattern. 'I wrote the word "incurable" in a razor blade down my arm,' Scott replied.

After the mid-morning break Sir David tried to demonstrate Scott was also dishonourable. He had been paid £2500 for letters, in return for which he had agreed to destroy his copies. But he had solicited photostats back from the journalist Gordon Winter. Scott eventually conceded: 'I agreed but then did not comply,' and tried to justify it. If he had no documents and because of his nervous condition, 'I could easily have been clapped into an institution and nobody would ever have believed a thing that I said.' Sir David tried vainly to interrupt the flow. 'I listen to you, Mr Scott.' Scott snapped back: 'Of course. That's what you're paid for.'

The wrangling went on for another twenty minutes. Eventually Sir David returned to Scott's health. Why had he been off drugs for the past three years? 'I think after the shooting I did not have to lie any more and it has just been absolutely marvellous. My life has been completely different.'

Sir David slid neatly into his next line of questioning. 'You have made a lot of money?' 'A little I earned by the sweat of my brow schooling horses.' How much had he made from the media? 'Vaguely about £1200 from August when Mr Thorpe was charged.' Before that he had been with the *Daily Mirror* at £1000 per day but after four days, 'I couldn't stand it. I wanted to get back to my horses.'

But he admitted that the previous day, Sunday, he signed a contract with Mirror Books, part of the newspaper group. Sir David was clearly upset at this lack of respect for the law. 'At the time you were giving evidence?' 'Yes. What difference does that make?' He had 'literally no idea' how much money he would get.

At the end of nearly nine hours of evidence Sir David started to wind up. 'Over a very long period of years you had been making these allegations about Mr Thorpe?' 'Yes.' . . . 'You are not really suggesting that you were regarded as a danger?' 'No. I think I became a danger though.'

Would he attribute all his problems to the Insurance cards? 'No, I would attribute a lot to the actual relationship because it really did upset me. It really screwed me up.'

But Sir David got his answer at the end. Scott admitted: 'Predominantly, yes, in my mind the Insurance cards.'

Taylor's re-examination was brief. He finished: 'Is the evidence you have given here true?' Scott replied: 'To the best of my knowledge, true. I have told the truth.'

8

Miller and others

Much had been heard of the South Wales connection:
one of the men involved, printer David Miller of Cardiff, was now produced as a major prosecution witness.
But his position was an odd one, as was soon to become
clear. 'Mr Miller should be given a warning,' Taylor
announced. Fred Winder, the clerk, solemnly told him:
'You are not bound to answer questions which would
incriminate you.'

For a silk-screen printer, Miller had a startling colour
sense: he arrived in court with a blue-grey suit, a grey-
pink wide-check shirt, and a large brown tie. Although
a contemporary of the 32-year-old gun-man Newton,
Miller's hair – bald on top, long behind – and his round,
heavy face, made him look older.

The affair started for Miller, he testified, when one of
his customers, George Deakin, asked him if he knew
anyone 'who would do anything for a laugh or a giggle
for money'. Miller thought of his old friend Andrew
Newton, who had earlier told the court he visited Miller
frequently to go to rugby matches at Cardiff Arms
Park.

Miller took Newton along to the Showman's dinner
in Blackpool and introduced him to Deakin. Newton
was drunk, and Miller took him home, where he was
sick on the bed. Miller briefly returned to the dinner.

Taylor moved Miller on to that autumn of 1975 and
the night of the dog-shooting. In his Cardiff office, after
midnight, he came upon Newton trying to release the

130

firing pin of his gun. 'He told me what had happened.'
Miller gave him emery cloth and oil, watching: 'I saw
him pull a bullet out from under the firing pin.' Newton
reassembled his gun and fired a shot into the wall. He
also had with him, Miller observed, an open briefcase, a
matchbox with bullets, a Polaroid camera and some
pink paper with writing on it.

Later Miller went to meet Newton in London, bringing the gun and the pink paper, which had been hidden
in a jiffy-bag in Miller's false ceiling. (Before leaving
Cardiff, Newton had fired a couple of further shots into
the shed door in the next-door garden.) The two men
were going on holiday with Newton's girl friend. At the
airport, Miller said he heard Newton ringing up
Deakin. 'Newton said he'd shot the dog, that everything
had gone wrong, and he was flying out of the country on
holiday.' Wasn't there anything else? Taylor prodded
him. (Newton had earlier recounted remarking to
Deakin: "The gun jammed."') Deakin's counsel leapt to
his feet. 'The witness has said quite plainly there was
nothing else.' Donati, the chairman of the Bench, made
one of his rare interventions: 'We'll leave it there,' he
told Taylor.

Newton and Miller were both interviewed by police
on their return from holiday in Karachi. Newton subsequently arrived in Cardiff with a tape-recorder and Miller decided to buy one of the same make. He used it
when Deakin rang him up while Newton was in jail.
Someone was coming to see him, Deakin told him, and
Miller rigged a microphone behind one of his box files.
The visitor was Le Mesurier, who showed him the note
initialled 'A.N.' to Holmes, apparently from Newton. 'I
said it wasn't his handwriting.' The 'bugged' conversation, later read into evidence by the Crown, went in
part like this:

LE MESURIER: '. . . all we want to do is, when Andrew
comes out everything is arranged. All the money is
ready for him. . . . the way we see it basically is this,

all the arrangements that we made with Andrew stand. We want Andrew to [inaudible] because if the press get hold of him he starts blabbering, you know what I'm talking about, the geezer involved in this lot is fucking Lord Goodman. . . . These writers have already had letters from Lord Goodman threatening them if they mention Holmes's name they will be sued for criminal libel, fucking slander. Not from some little solicitor tucked away . . . Lord Goodman's office so they ain't playing with the boys you know, they have got the money, the real money to go up, so these two geezers who reckon they are going to write this book start any nonsense with Holmes in it, he will hit on to three things . . . *Private Eye* fucking closed *Private Eye* as you probably know. Well the same thing applies here we think, as it happens, so don't bother your bugs about the press. . . .'

MILLER: '. . . people are just so near the truth . . .'

LE MESURIER: 'Well it's like the cops saying, you know, they sit there and tell you they know all kind of things. They know nothing . . . . Let me put it to you in a proposition to you, say for what, do you want half hundred, hundred quid to go up there?'

MILLER: 'Mmm.'

LE MESURIER: 'To see him, so I drive you up there in me motor and you go and see him, tell him it's all right. We want him reassured, you see . . . .'

MILLER: 'What we, you told me, he was in for ten grand.'

LE MESURIER: 'That's right, it is all ready for him, I mean if he came tomorrow and said . . . ten Gs, well I guess he knows it is all put to one side and it's all ready . . . if I may pursue it a little bit further with you, bear with me, what you know, Andrew. I have never met him you know what [inaudible] he would, take the ten grand on the deal.'

MILLER: 'Yeah.'

LE MESURIER: 'And forget about it.'

MILLER: 'Yep.'

LE MESURIER: '. . . whatever Andrew wants in Hong Kong, that can be arranged . . . ten grand could buy it . . . you are not talking about people with a few bob you know, I mean these people have got a good lot of money, I mean ten grand was up like that . . . as long as you can convey to Andrew the fact that you know everyone is going to stand by what they said, and bend over backwards to help him . . . they'd set him up you know, I mean set him up, no fucking about, that's it you know. They don't want any nonsense with the press no books no nothing . . . .'

MILLER: '. . . you know after the court case there was a big thing in the front page.'

LE MESURIER: 'What was that about?'

MILLER: 'Oh with the gun. He came up here that night cleaning the thing out.'

LE MESURIER: 'What did he do that for?'

MILLER: 'Well he said it had jammed. You know what he's like, he pulls everything to bits. "Why hasn't it fucking worked? File! Give me this, give me some oil," then we were downstairs, then firing into the bushes. "Oh, the fucking thing is working now," you know.'

LE MESURIER: 'I must say my only observation of things, I thought he was rather silly going taking his own fucking motor.'

MILLER: 'He is stupid altogether . . . the press seem to think that he was paid to mess it up by the South Africans . . . just to get publicity for nothing or get publicity for the wrong reasons.'

LE MESURIER: 'So they don't suspect a real reason . . .?'

MILLER: 'Well some do, some don't.. . .'

LE MESURIER: 'I can certainly make arrangements for you to get a lot of fucking business . . . just phone Donald from a business point of view I mean.'

MILLER: 'Who is it, Donald who then?'

LE MESURIER: 'I'm sorry he is not Don, he is George Deakin . . . if he [Newton] gets his money and the [inaudible] that was arranged, he is not going to go the other way is he?'

MILLER: 'No, he loves money, Andrew.'

LE MESURIER: 'Yeah.'

MILLER: 'That's his problem.'

LE MESURIER: 'Ten Gs tax-free ain't bad, is it?'

MILLER: 'Wish I had it you know.'

LE MESURIER: '. . . so all you have got to do is, we think at this stage, is reassure him so that if these buggers get at him, you know, as soon as he comes out. . . .'

MILLER: 'He can't do that can he, you know that as well as I do . . . he would be done for attempted murder you see.'

LE MESURIER: 'Fucking bastard. I said that to Don, I said to him that he can't do anything about it. I said they will do him, they will put him away. He said they can't charge you for the same thing twice. I said, fuck off they will have him for attempted murder, they didn't do that with him before.'

Miller also taped a subsequent conversation on the phone with Deakin:

DEAKIN: 'Dave, hello.'

MILLER: '. . . I don't want to say too much on the phone. Say the guy last night . . . what he wants to do is to go up.'

DEAKIN: 'Next week.'

MILLER: 'Next week, and try to see him . . . . Who is that guy? OK? It's on the level is it? . . . I am not being set up for something?'

DEAKIN: 'No, no, I wouldn't do that to you.'

MILLER: 'You know the way he said: "I'll give you a lift back in my car," and you know, sort of, you know, "Out-on-the-moors" touch.'

DEAKIN: 'No, no, they wouldn't . . . it's very genuine Dave.'

MILLER: '. . . he is going to give me a ring on, er, Monday. Will you see him before then?'

DEAKIN: 'Yes. Seeing him Friday.'

MILLER: '. . . You know what I mean, there is so much going on, you don't know who's who, do you?'

DEAKIN: 'No, no.'

On 6 April 1977 Newton was released from prison. 'He got in touch with me,' Miller said. He told Le Mesurier. 'Arrangements were made to pay Newton the £5000.' A tape recording of a phone conversation with Le Mesurier was read into the evidence by the Crown later. Extracts from it ran like this:

MILLER: 'Yeah.'

LE MESURIER: 'John.'

MILLER: 'Hello, how are you?'

LE MESURIER: 'All right. Just the arrangements that have been made with Newton . . . look would it be convenient for you to bring him somewhere and meet altogether . . . let's think, I know a lovely place where no one will ever see us . . . it's on a common at Brides or somewhere like that.'

MILLER: 'St Brides. . .'

LE MESURIER: '. . . I'll tell you what to do. Come to the Pelican Inn right. . . . Right, I'll be there with a car and I'll drive on in front of you OK? . . . so as you come up the road flash your lights . . . if you come to the Pelican and there is anyone following you, um, what can we do?'

MILLER: 'Well.'

LE MESURIER: 'Just flash your lights twice.'

MILLER: 'Yeah.'

LE MESURIER: 'But don't flash them on the switch, flash them on the flasher otherwise the back lights light up. . . . I'll stay there for an hour until five o'clock. . . . Then I'll go back to me office . . . with the five Gs he won't go flashing it around will he?'

MILLER: '. . . He is very mean.'

LE MESURIER: '. . . Good, well I hope he isn't going to

go out down Savile Row and buy himself some flash suit and a flash car and all that you know.'

MILLER: '. . . you said five? . . . What? Was that the arrangement was it?'

LE MESURIER: 'Oh yeah, I spoken to my friends . . . I mean I did think it was twice as much . . . and they said oh no it ain't, it's five you know that was all arranged, so there is no problem with him about that, they said, because he knows how much it is.... That's super Dave, thanks for all your trouble.'

Miller was to get £100 for his part in arranging the pay-off and engaged a private detective agency, Dabs of Cardiff, to photograph the meeting. 'I just wanted to protect myself,' Miller said. At St Brides Common, Le Mesurier had panicked when he saw a girl photographer in a car that drove past. 'He said: "Let's get out of here. They've got a photograph of us that will link me with Holmes."' Miller drove Newton back after the pay-off at the brickworks, and dropped him at Cardiff General station. When they arrived, Newton had still not finished counting bundles of £5 notes.

Later Miller met Le Mesurier, who told him Holmes, who was in Denmark, was interested in knowing what was going on. Le Mesurier was worried about the photographer, and said Newton had gone to South Africa on an airline ticket he had bought him. 'He was going to be there for a long time,' Le Mesurier remarked. Miller later phoned Deakin. A transcript of this conversation was also read into the evidence later. These are extracts from it:

MILLER: 'Hello.'

DEAKIN: 'Dave?'

MILLER: 'Yes, George.'

DEAKIN: 'Heard anything?'

MILLER: 'Yeah bad news really.... Big article on me....'

DEAKIN: 'Anything on me?'

MILLER: 'Nothing but it's er Newton's made a statement with his solicitor to the papers.'

DEAKIN: 'Yes.'

MILLER: 'He is going to name everybody you know why he has done it, it is obviously money.'

DEAKIN: 'Yes, well I'm denying, what are you going to do?'

MILLER: 'Well you know um um I'm just going to look after myself if it comes down to it . . . why has he fucking done it?'

DEAKIN: 'I don't know.'

MILLER: 'You know didn't somebody come up with the goodies, or what?'

DEAKIN: 'Yes, yes, they came up with that.'

MILLER: '. . . You seen a solicitor?'

DEAKIN: 'Well, I have seen mine.'

MILLER: 'Yeah.'

DEAKIN: 'And as I said to him that, as far as I am concerned, they just wanted somebody to frighten somebody.'

*   *   *   *   *

MILLER: 'He says there he has admitted a story about how he tried to shoot Scott that night but he, you know, he couldn't do it and pointed the gun away to frighten him.'

DEAKIN: 'Um.'

MILLER: 'He didn't, you know, he didn't say that he pointed the gun at his head and it stuck or anything like that, so he is lying again.'

DEAKIN: 'Yes um . . . I don't like speaking too much on the phone.'

*   *   *   *   *

MILLER: 'Yeah, and they don't, they don't know anything about, you know, all the other details he had from you and all that sort of thing.'

137

DEAKIN: 'No nothing, I didn't, you know, nothing at all.'

*　　*　　*　　*　　*

MILLER: '. . . But, you know, when it comes to it he might, you know, with details, you know, how do, you know, then all this he will be mentioning your name, he mentioned you give him photographs and all this sort of rubbish, you know. If he can get himself out of it he will.'

DEAKIN: 'Well, there is nothing for him to, the only thing he can earn out of it is money, see, you know, he won't, nothing else can happen to him, nothing at all.'

MILLER: '. . . the last time I heard was that they are being made to look fools aren't they, the police? If it all comes out they are going to really go into it.'

DEAKIN: 'Yes, but there is such a lot of high powers at the moment trying to hush it up still.'

MILLER: 'Yeah well hopefully yeah.'

DEAKIN: 'Yeah there is as it happens and this is genuine . . . .'

MILLER: 'OK George.'

DEAKIN: 'Ta Ta.'

MILLER: 'See you.'

Gareth Williams, QC for Deakin, was the first to cross-examine. Would Miller agree that over the years he had known Deakin he had found him to be 'a generous, open-hearted person'? Miller hesitated. 'A businessman,' he said, eventually. There was laughter. He then agreed that 'socially' Deakin was generous.

Miller denied that Deakin had ever talked to him about someone being blackmailed, a lady who had already committed suicide, and the life of a small child being threatened.

Williams turned to the by-now-notorious Showman's dinner. Miller said by the end of the evening Newton was 'absolutely drunk'. 'I had to carry him to the car and drive him home. Earlier he had been drinking from a bottle of brandy. There were topless dancers . . . .' Williams interrupted, with a sigh: 'I thought we'd get to that.' Miller continued: 'Newton had his own bottle of brandy and got into a fight.'

Miller stoutly denied the truth of Newton's statement that he himself had been 'a prime mover' in putting him in touch with people who wanted someone eliminated. 'I found Newton to be a habitual liar before these matters.' He said: 'I am sure he *can* tell fact from fantasy. He just tells lies anyway.' Miller added: 'We called him "Chicken-brain". . . . He told me about parties with prominent persons involved, members of the House of Lords and prominent political persons. He always had an incredible story every time you saw him.'

Williams turned to money. Miller's attention was temporarily distracted as an unseasonal tortoise-shell butterfly made its way erratically across the courtroom. He agreed he had had £500 from the *Daily Mirror*, who had also paid his expenses to sit through Newton's original trial at Exeter.

He had received a much larger sum – £8000 – from the *People* in June or July of 1977. But he denied that he had carefully taped conversations with Deakin in order to sell the tapes. Later, he conceded he had received another £500 from various television companies, including £50 from BBC Wales for a simulation of the £5000 pay-off meeting at St Brides. He regarded it as adequate repayment 'for the time spend dodging newspapers'.

Miller said he tried to give what he described as his 'volatile package' of tape-recordings and photographs to the police. But when he rang, they said they could not see him for five days. 'It was like trying to make an appointment with the dentist.' So the next day he instead contacted the *People*. 'They offered the money. I did not want the £8000, so I even asked my solicitor to offer it to the blind school.' It never got there. Miller had saved it instead. 'It was never my intention to sell my story to the paper,' he emphasized. 'The package was purely and simply insurance.' He amplified this point in a brief re-examination by Taylor for the Crown, when he said he had deposited the tapes with his solicitor and 'provided myself with a certain amount of insurance in case anything happened to me. Not that it would do any good, but it was on record.' Miller said the *People* story 'achieved what I set out to do and got the story out – but only after Newton had first brought it out'.

The Crown now produced a man called Colin Lambert to reinforce their evidence against Le Mesurier. Lambert was outside sales manager for Le Mesurier's Pyle Carpet Discount Centre, and said that in the autumn of 1977, he had asked Le Mesurier if he had paid the £5000. By then the payment had been in the newspapers. 'He said yes, he had paid that money.' As they walked to the car from Lambert's house, 'Le Mesurier said something to the effect that "Davie says we're going to jail."'

About six weeks later, when Le Mesurier had retired from the firm 'so that none of the smut or dirt would be reflected on it', Lambert met him again. 'He said to me a fool had been hired to kill Norman Scott and someone more like myself should have been hired to do the job.' Lambert was most concerned the press should not get the idea that he was 'some man from Detroit who goes round shooting people'. He addressed himself directly to the press benches and explained this was a reference to his having been in two Welsh Infantry Regiments for sixteen and a half years. He had remarked earlier that only an idiot would go and try to shoot someone with a gun that did not work.

A £169,000 football pools winner now swam briefly in and out of the Thorpe case. Terry Gibbs, a former Welsh miner, testified in a written statement that he had been advised on how to invest his winnings by David Holmes himself. Holmes introduced him to Le Mesurier – 'it was evident they knew each other well' – and Holmes told him to give Le Mesurier a £10,000 interest-free loan in March 1976. Gibbs went on to invest more in Le Mesurier's firm and became a partner in the carpet centre, although 'John Le Mesurier virtually ran the business'. Le Mesurier told him in 1977 that although press reports were not true, he might end in prison.

Gibbs's written evidence was one of 28 from various minor Crown witnesses that were read into the case. The minor witnesses, some merely experts concerned with subjects like authenticating tape-recordings, were not considered important enough, or not contested, so there was no need for the Crown to actually call in person more than the ten who gave evidence and were cross-examined.

The committal proceedings now took a sudden leap in time, away from evidence of a final 'cover-up', and back to that Devon Christmas seventeen years ago when, according to Scott, Thorpe took him into the green-tiled bathroom of the Broomhills Hotel and made love to him as Thorpe's mother walked around the garden outside with Jimmy and Mary Collier.

The Colliers came separately to the witness box: they each now owned hotels in different parts of the country. But then, in 1961, they lived together in Devon, and James Collier was the prospective Liberal candidate for Tiverton. Both remembered Scott staying with them that Christmas, at Thorpe's request, and both remembered the Broomhills lunch and the walk round the garden, leaving Thorpe and Scott behind.

Scott's story was that Thorpe told the Colliers Scott was going upstairs to try on a shirt. James Collier testified: 'After lunch Mr Thorpe said he had some shirts which might fit Norman.'

Scott also maintained he stayed that night with Thorpe. James Collier said he thought Scott returned home with them that evening. Mrs Collier could not remember. Mrs Collier did remember Scott arriving 'out of the blue' in 1962 at the Easton Hotel in Victoria, where she was working as a receptionist. Miss Caroline Barrington-Ward came, and also the police. 'I had nothing to do with that.' And James Collier remembered, in summer or autumn 1965, the arrival of Bessell, who discussed Scott with him in Exeter, telling him about the Dublin letter to Mrs Ursula Thorpe, and that homosexual allegations were being made.

Sir David put it to both the Colliers individually that it was the police who had 'put into their minds' the idea of their walk round the hotel grounds after lunch.

Sir David: 'Did he [the police officer] suggest to you, you went for a walk?' Mrs Collier: 'No, I remember myself we went for a walk in the garden.'

Sir David: 'The walk in the garden – was it put to you by the police?' James Collier: 'I don't think the police put it to me.' Sir David: 'You wouldn't have volunteered that. . .' James Collier [disagreeing]: 'I don't know . . . I remembered it . . . he asked me what happened during lunch and after.'

Mrs Collier was definite, however, that Scott never discussed his personal life with her, and never discussed having a quarrel with Thorpe. Mr Collier was quoted in a *Daily Mail* interview in which he said Bessell talked about going to Ireland to see Scott, at the Exeter meeting. He thought Bessell had not been to Ireland at that point, Collier said. When Taylor, re-examining for the Crown, asked Collier, of the homosexual relationship: 'Did Scott every say anything to you?' Sir David sprang to his feet and objected: 'I can't see how that arises out of cross-examination.' Donati, the chairman, overruled him. 'No, he hadn't ever said anything to me about it,' Collier replied.

Their evidence finished, the Colliers left separately. Mrs Collier added another entry for the number plate spotters who had already jotted down WAD 7 – the personalized plate bought by Deakin for his wife,

Wendy, and bolted to a dark blue Mercedes saloon. Mrs Collier had a number for a hotel proprietor on her coral pink BMW – BAR 2.

9

The police

Detective Chief Superintendent Michael John Challes
was the last Crown witness. He took the oath with the
practised ease of twenty six years as a police officer, and
agreed that he was a member of the Avon and Somerset
Constabulary, stationed at Bristol. Taylor started by
producing Challes's fourteen page statement, made on
5 September 1978. Challes fished his glasses out of his
pocket, and stood solidly in the box turning the pages as
Taylor read it out. The statement was basically a
chronological list of the police enquiries.

At 4.35 p.m. on 26 October 1977 Challes had gone
to West Drayton police station to see Andrew Gino
Newton who he had taken to Bristol, and then interviewed for three days. At 1.45 a.m. on 29 October, his
junior officer Detective Superintendent David
Greenough had returned to Bristol with an envelope
'found to contain Bank of England notes of various
denominations'. They totalled £3060. On 1 December,
Challes had gone to Cardiff where he saw David Miller,
who handed him seven cassette tapes, two colour
photographs and negatives, four black-and-white negatives and prints, documents, a copy cheque, a tape-
recorder, and a telephone-tapping device. Challes had
gone to 'premises at the rear' where Miller had indicated where there had once been a shed into which
Newton had fired shots. It had now been demolished.
Miller had also showed him where a gun had been con-
cealed. With Miller's solicitor the two had then gone to
St Brides Common at Ogmore-on-Sea, where Miller

had pointed out where Newton had met Le Mesurier.

On 15 November Challes had interviewed Deakin in Port Talbot. Deakin's solicitor had handed him a prepared statement. It said he had known Le Mesurier since the 1970s, and his only contact with him had been social. In 1973 Le Mesurier had introduced Homes to him as a tax consultant. At the second meeting about tax matters, Deakin said, as they were getting up to leave, Le Mesurier mentioned a friend of his, who was being blackmailed. There was talk of a woman who had committed suicide, and threats against the life of a three-year-old child. He wanted to know if there was anybody who could frighten the blackmailer off. "'It was raised almost casually. I asked why they did not go to the police.'" The answer was: "'Well, it's one of those cases where you can't.'" Deakin said he was friendly with Miller, and mentioned the conversation to him. He remembered saying: "'Isn't it awful, somebody threatening a three-year-old for money?'" Miller and he had gone to the Amusement Trade Exhibition in Blackpool where, at the Savoy, Miller introduced him to Newton and said that he was perhaps the bloke who could help him out. "'I repeated to Newton what I had been told.'" Deakin said he imagined they were looking for "'a burly type and an ex-boxer'" and Newton was not that sort. He had thought no more about it.

Two days after he returned to Port Talbot Newton phoned, and asked if he was serious. Deakin said he did not know much, and gave him the telephone number of Holmes in Manchester. A short time after, he met Newton accidentally and Newton said to him: "'Who are these bloody people you introduced me to? They sent me to Dunstable, and there is no such street there.'" Deakin had never had any contact with Newton again. Miller had since related various parts of the story to him, but he said: "'I am in such a position I do not know who or what to believe.'"

The court now went through another charade to reconstruct the questioning that followed the statement. Taylor played Deakin, and Challes played himself, Deakin denying that he had said he wanted "'someone to bump someone off'", and that he had met Newton at the Aust service station and given him the album of photographs. Deakin supposed Holmes was to give Newton his instructions. Miller had talked to him, when Newton had been jailed. "'He said there was money to be paid, and even mentioned Harold Wilson and Jeremy Thorpe.'"

Challes's statement went through a series of interviews in the New Year of 1978. On 9 and 18 January he had seen Scott. On 24 January he went to the newspaper publishers, IPC, and collected 'copies of correspondence and a letter to Mrs Ursula Thorpe' from them. (The *Sunday Mirror* editor, Robert Edwards, had told the court earlier in a written statement that he got the Dublin letter and other material from workmen cleaning out Bessell's former Pall Mall offices. The *Sunday Mirror* went to Thorpe and handed the discoveries over in November 1974. They also photocopied much of the contents and locked them in their legal department's safe. The workmen themselves testified that a £200 cheque later arrived from the paper: they shared it out between them.) On 1 March Challes interviewed Newton again at Bristol, and played tapes to him. Between 6 and 10 March he had interviewed Bessell in California, and taken two letters (from Thorpe to Bessell), correspondence, and 'the Lloyd George book'.

On 3 April, he had seen Holmes at his London flat and taken him to Bristol, with his solicitor. Over the next two days, Holmes had been interviewed at length. He replied to only a few questions, answering: "'No comment'" to the others. Practically all the 'replies' were withdrawn when he was next interviewed. Holmes said he had known Thorpe over twenty nine years, and Dinshaw between seven and eight years. He described Hayward as "'an acquaintance'". He said that in February 1974, he had been involved in the purchase of letters written from Bessell to Scott, and paid £2500 by cheque drawn on his personal account. "'Were you reimbursed for that payment by anyone else?'" Challes asked. Holmes replied: "'No.'" He had thought that, two days before the election, the letters "'could be very damaging'". Challes asked him if he agreed £2500 was a lot to pay. Holmes said, from a historian's viewpoint, the Zinoviev letter had a great effect on the 1924 election. "'The fact a Liberal MP had been paying regular sums concerned me.'" Challes told him: "'I suggest Thorpe was being troubled by Scott and you were helping, even to the extent of being involved in a conspiracy to murder.'" Holmes replied: "'No comment,'" although he accepted that he had no personal grievance against Scott, who he said earlier in the interview he did not know.

At the same time, Le Mesurier was also brought to Bristol Central police station where he said he had nothing to say and declined to go on an identity parade. Both men were released after Challes had played a copy of a tape to Holmes and asked: "'Is that you on the other end?'" Holmes had replied: "'No comment at all.'"

A week later, on 12 April, Challes interviewed Deakin again for three hours. He again denied meeting Newton at Aust service station or showing him the album. He said he had never met Scott, visited Barnstable, or been involved in the taking of documents. Challes had said to him: "'I am suggesting your interest and involvement was much deeper.'" Deakin had replied: "'Not so.'" "'I was told by Le Mesurier, others were involved including David Holmes and prominent politicians,'" Deakin said. He denied he had been involved in the 'pay-off arrangements'.

The next morning, Thursday and day 13 of the hearings, it was John Bull who stood up instead of Taylor. He read a statement by Chief Inspector Brian McCreery of the Devon and Cornwall Constabulary, based at Barnstable. McCreery, with Detective Chief

Superintendent Proven Sharpe, had carried out the
original investigation in 1976 into the shooting of
Scott's dog and on 8 February that year had interviewed Thorpe at his home. Thorpe had made a statement to the two officers which Bull read to the court. It
ran:

'I am the member of Parliament for the North Devon constituency. I am in the process of drafting a comprehensive
statement relating to my knowledge of Mr Norman Josiffe,
otherwise known as Norman Scott, which, subject to the
advice of my legal advisers, I would have no objection to
supplying to those investigating this case. At this stage I have
been interviewed on three specific points.

'First, Mr Michael Barnes, solicitor, of The Square, Barnstaple. Mr Barnes has acted for me on a variety of business
matters connected with my affairs in North Devon, in particular the purchase of my present house, the negotiation of a
mortgage, the purchase of land belonging to my neighbours,
and a number of other matters.

'With regard to the Scott affair, to the best of my know-
ledge and belief, the only instruction which I gave to Mr
Barnes was to warn my then Conservative opponent, Mr
Keigwin, in either the 1970 or 1974 elections, that were the
Scott matter to be raised, I would unquestionably issue a writ
for defamation.

'Apart from this, I have no recollection of giving Mr Barnes
any further instructions on any matter relating to this. I have
been asked whether I would object to Mr Barnes disclosing
information which came to him in the course of his professional activities which could in any way be construed to affect
or involve myself and Scott.

'While this is obviously a matter for him to determine,
speaking for myself I would have no conceivable objection.

'Secondly, I have been asked for information I can produce
relating to the alleged payment of £2500 in respect of certain
letters and/or documents.

'Of this particular transaction I have no knowledge whatsoever. However, I do believe that Dr Gleadle made contact
with Mr (now Lord) Banks around December 1973, or January 1974, indicating he, Dr Gleadle, was in possession of
documents, which could be embarrassing for the Liberal Party

and which the Liberal Party might wish to possess.

'Lord Banks consulted Lord Wade. Lord Wade, at my suggestion, consulted the Liberal leader in the Lords, Lord Byers, who closely questioned Lord Banks as to whether Gleadle's suggestion was that either the documents be handed over, or bought.

'On this point Lord Banks was uncertain. At a later date, which can be confirmed by consulting my office engagements diary, I was visited by the Rector of North Molton, who asked me whether I knew of a Norman Scott who was making serious allegations against me.

'He alluded to the fact that there existed correspondence which could prove embarrassing either to me, Mr Peter Bessell, the Liberal Party, or all three. He also suggested that the Liberal Party might like to 'set up' this young man financially and indicated that he felt that Scott's over-riding purpose was to destroy me.

'He mentioned that he and Dr Gleadle, both of whom had been treating Scott over a period of time, were anxious to form a trust to set him up in some form of business, such as a riding establishment.

'I concede that this conversation could be construed as a veiled attempt at blackmail but knowing that Pennington's (the rector) motive was to try to help Scott, to whom he administered both as a priest and as a member of the Samaritans, I did not so interpret it, although I robustly rejected the suggestion that I or any of my colleagues should be involved in these "good works".

'I replied that I was certain that neither the Liberal Party nor myself nor Mr Bessell would have any interest in so assisting. I also indicated that I should be surprised if the documents to which he alluded differed materially from those which my colleagues had examined in 1971, to which I had immediate access to photostat and further photostats of which I believed were already in the possession of certain newspapers, none of which occasioned me concern.

'I have not spoken to the vicar since. I should add that I have never seen Dr Gleadle, never corresponded with him, never spoken to him on the telephone nor had any communication with him, direct or indirect.

'The third and final point relates to the reported incident of the dog on Exmoor on October 24, 1975. I have never met the accused, Mr Newton, I have never seen him, direct or indirect. In respect of this incident I again know no more than I have read in the press.'

McCreery said about the 'comprehensive statement' mentioned in the first paragraph of Thorpe's statement: "'A copy has as far as I know never been received by the Devon and Cornwall Constabulary.'" Proven Sharpe had also seen Holmes at the Reform Club in London, but he had declined to make a statement.

Challes then continued his chronological account of events. On 10 May 1978, he had interviewed Holmes at his request in the offices of the solicitors D. J. Freeman in Cavendish Square, London. Holmes had handed him a prepared, but unsigned, statement in which he substituted: "'No comment'" for his few previous answers. Challes had put a further series of questions to him to which again he had replied: "'No comment'" to all. Five days later, on 15 May, Challes interviewed Jack Hayward, who handed him a letter written by Thorpe.

Thorpe was interviewed on 3 June at Bath police station in the presence of his solicitor, Sir David Napley. Sir David had handed him a prepared statement, already signed. The long statement was then read out in court:

'I have been informed by my solicitors that it has been indicated that the current investigation covers three main areas. The first is whether I had ever been involved in a homosexual relationship with Norman Josiffe, also known as Norman Scott, which might form a motive or a wish on my part to eliminate him, cause him injury, or put him in fear.

'The second is whether I had been a party to any conspiracy to kill or injure him or put him in fear. The third, whether I had paid or authorized any payment to one Newton, or any other person, pursuant to or following upon, any such conspiracy, or to Scott in respect of the purchase of certain documents or otherwise.

'In October 1977, I made a statement to the press. I now wish to reiterate and confirm as accurate what I said in that statement, save as to certain minor details which are dealt with in the body of this statement and also to add the following:

'As to the first allegation, I wish, with all the emphasis I can command, to deny that I was at any time engaged in any homosexual relationships with Scott or that I was at any time a party to any homosexual familiarity with him.

'I described in my earlier statement, and have here confirmed, the circumstances under which I met Scott. I believed that he was a person who was desperately in need of help and support, in that he was in a suicidal and unbalanced state.

'The action which, in the circumstances, I followed was attributable solely to what I saw as my duty, having regard to the conditions under which he approached me; in the event my compassion and kindness towards him was in due course repaid with malevolence and resentment.

'Although he never so informed me, I formed the opinion at an early stage on the limited number of occasions I was in his presence, that he was a homosexual and he was becoming too dependent upon me.

'Accordingly, I made immediate arrangements for him to be accepted into a family near Tiverton with whom he was to spend Christmas, having explained to them the reasons why I believed he was in need of help.

'However, after only a few weeks in their house they decided his highly neurotic and unbalanced state was too disturbing an influence in the house and he was asked to leave.

'At about January 1962, Scott was still in an unsettled state and in need of funds to enable him to establish some means of supporting himself. He had informed me that his father had been killed in an air crash in South America and I suggested that it might be possible to obtain some compensation.

'Accordingly I requested a solicitor friend to initiate some inquiries. In due course, he informed me the story told by Scott was quite false. In fact, his father was at that time, a hospital porter living in Bexleyheath in Kent, where his mother also lived.

'I told him there was nothing further I could do to help. He became highly excited and emotional. The meeting itself lasted no longer than a quarter of an hour. Subsequently, he sought to see me again in 1963 expressing contrition and asking me to allow him to meet me and seek my forgiveness.

'I arranged to meet him and did so publicly on the terrace

of the House of Commons, at which meeting he again became highly excited and emotional but, before leaving, suggested I owed him some duty to support him financially, which I refuted in forceful terms.

'With hindsight I now realize that my proper course would have been to refuse to see him. It was evident from our last meeting that he resented my disinterest in him and was likely to try to cause trouble.

'I was on the horns of a dilemma. I foresaw no problem in resisting any demands which he might make upon me and disproving falsehoods which he might offer against me.

'However, I suspected that the allegations at which he was hinting, although without the slightest foundation, were such as would involve, as in the event they have, baring my soul in public which could have, however unfairly, serious political implications and repercussions for me and the Liberal Party.

'As a result I misguidedly agreed to see him and did so on one further occasion, which I think was at my flat. I agreed to this meeting in the belief that it was better to avoid public discussion and that I could convince him that his grievances were wholly unjustified and fanciful.

'As to the second allegation I wish, with no less emphasis, entirely to refute any suggestion that I have at any time been a party to any conspiracy to kill or injure Norman Scott, or to put him in fear, or that at any time I had any knowledge of, or believed in the existence of, any such conspiracy.

'Quite apart from the fact that any desire or willingness to kill or cause physical harm to any person is wholly alien to my nature, as many would be prepared to confirm, the circumstances which existed at the time when it was subsequently suggested that such a conspiracy may have existed are wholly inconsistent with the pursuit of the alleged objective of such a conspiracy.

'As I have mentioned above, there was a period when I was understandably concerned at the political implications which could result from the wild and unfounded allegations which it seemed probable that Norman Scott would publish.

'As I have further explained, my disquiet in that connection was in no way attributable to my having in any way been involved in any homosexual relationships with him, but because I foresaw that the mere necessity of truthfully denying such an association might raise, as a matter of public question, my own private matters wholly unconnected with

Scott, which in my view I could claim to be private to me alone.

'It has been suggested in a recently published book that the time the alleged conspiracy was conceived and embarked upon was in the spring of 1975. By that time Scott had ensured in a variety of ways, including a statement in the course of an inquest in 1973 [the inquest was in fact in May 1972], that his allegations had been widely disseminated and, although fully known by the press and the major political parties, wisely ignored by them.

'The worst that Scott could falsely allege had been revealed. Far from this having adversely affected either me or the Liberal Party politically, which had been my fear, the party under my leadership, had increased its vote in two elections in February and October 1974 from 2 millions to 6 millions and 5½ millions respectively and I had increased my own majority from 369 to 11,000 and 6700 respectively.

'Against this background it is manifestly ludicrous to suggest either that I any longer considered that any public reliance would be placed upon the utterances of Scott, or that any measures were needed to deal with him, least of all the wholly unthinkable approach of conspiring to achieve his death, injury or otherwise.

'It appears that Newton was responsible for causing the death of Scott's dog and may have made an abortive attempt upon the life of Scott. I do not pretend to know the truth of this matter and I can only reassert that not only did I have no need to take any part in any such project, and did not do so, but I had no knowledge whatsoever of it and was not, and would not, have under any circumstances have been willing to allow any such plot to be pursued had any hint of suggestion come to me about it.

'Finally, in relation to the third allegation, I wish vigorously to refute any suggestion that at any time I had knowingly been a party, either directly or indirectly, to the payment of any such money whatsoever to Newton or to Scott for the purpose alleged.

'The press have reported that the payment of £2500 was made indirectly to Norman Scott in February 1974, for the delivery of certain letters and documents which had passed between him and others, not including myself.

'I understand that it is claimed a sum of £5000 had been paid to Newton subsequent to the death of Scott's dog after his release from prison and that the second sum had been dispersed from moneys provided by one Jack Hayward.

'I had no knowledge whatsoever of the purchase of the letters in question until the early part of 1976 when the fact was first publicly revealed in the national press. I immediately expressed, and continue to express, both my surprise and indeed my horror that any one could have thought it necessary to embark upon such a course.

'The letters had already been widely circulated and indeed seen by my parliamentary colleagues in 1971.

'I have no personal knowledge whatsoever of any payment to Newton of the sum of £5000, or otherwise, and at no time made any arrangements for any such payments. It is correct that Mr Hayward paid me personally two sums of £10,000, each of which was to be used by me in any way which I thought appropriate in relation to campaigning expenses.

'In fact, by reason of other donations at other times it became unnecessary to have recourse to these sums. There had been grave difficulties at one stage in raising sufficient money for the expenses for the Liberal Party's election campaign and I accordingly resolved that since Mr Hayward had made it quite plain to me that, not being an adherent to the Liberal Party, he was not making these moneys available to the party but to me personally, I would not cause them to be paid into the Liberal Party fund, where they would be soon defrayed.

'I therefore made arrangements for the sum of £20,000 to be deposited with accountants and to be held as an iron reserve against any shortage of funds at any subsequent election. At no time, however, have I ever authorized the use of these funds for any payment of the kind alleged to either Scott or Newton.

'I have in consultation with my legal advisers given long and earnest consideration as to whether I should amplify the firm and precise general denial set out above. They are conscious, as I am, of the fact that those who have in the past been minded to put forward false assertions against me have, from time to time, varied the detail of their account in order to adjust it to such hard facts as, from time to time, have emerged.

'Having regard to the unusual way in which these current allegations have emerged, there is a real danger that if specific details relating to matters which can be proved are made known at the present time they may, in the course of the investigation, become known to, or be deduced by, those minded to further the allegations with consequent readjustment of their version.

'In these circumstances, I have been advised that, whilst it is right and proper that I should re-express the denials which are contained in this statement, it is neither incumbent upon me nor desirable to add anything further.'

Challes told the court he had read the statement and then asked a number of questions. '"First, do you know David Holmes?"' Thorpe had replied that solely for reasons advised by his solicitor he should not add anything more to the statement. When all the other questions were put to him he said he made the same reply. '"Perhaps I could say: 'Ditto,'"' he said.' He proceeded to reply '"ditto"' to every question.

On 2 August 1978 Challes had obtained warrants for the arrest of all four, and on 4 August they had come to Minehead police station. Le Mesurier, Holmes and Deakin had made no reply when they were cautioned and charged. Thorpe when cautioned said: '"I hear what you say. I am totally innocent of these charges and will vigorously challenge them."' Challes finished off by saying that, following the court proceedings and the arresting and charging of the four defendants, he had obtained an order to inspect Holmes's account at the Midland Bank in Manchester, which he had since done.

Gareth Williams, for Deakin, started cross-examination immediately on the tack which was to preoccupy the defence lawyers – Challes's relationships with Pencourt. Challes agreed that in December 1977 he had flown to California to interview Bessell on the same aeroplane as Penrose and Courtiour. 'I did not know they were going to be on the same plane until I boarded it.' It was true he had had a number of interviews with Bessell in California and that Pencourt had been present. Williams: 'The material from the interviews forms the basis of his witness statement in this case.' Was it, Williams asked, a unique occurrence 'dur-

ing the whole of your vast experience as a police officer'
to have the journalists present? 'Yes sir.'

'Was that unique situation brought about because Mr
Bessell would not be interviewed by you unless these
two other gentlemen were there?' asked Williams. 'Yes
sir.' 'I am making no criticism of you, but I simply want
to establish the genesis of this matter,' Williams said.

Williams then, amid laughter in court, said he wanted
to return from California to 'a more civilized part of the
world' – South Wales. Had Challes not found that
Deakin answered every question? Challes after an ini-
tial hesitation, agreed that 'he has always answered the
questions in some manner. He has never said: "No
comment" or, "Ditto."' Williams wanted to know
about the prosecution witness, David Miller. Was he
not a man with previous convictions for violence and
dishonesty? Challes admitted police records showed
that he had been convicted for maliciously wounding a
police officer in 1972, and for obtaining an airline ticket
by deception in 1975. He agreed that as late as June
1978 Miller had still been regarded as a possible defendant in the case.

Michael Burton, Mathew's junior, for Holmes, the
next to question Challes, asked him if his client was a
man of 'impeccable character'. Challes agreed. Burton
then turned again to Pencourt. When Holmes had been
interviewed at his flat in London on 3 April, had Penrose and Courtiour been with Challes? 'They were in
the area because they had showed us where Mr Holmes
lived,' Challes replied. He had telephoned a number of
people. 'Penrose and Courtiour did not give the
address. They would not give it to me. They offered to
take us [Challes and Greenough] and point out the
house where he was residing. It was my only way of
getting in touch with Holmes and it was the best way.'

The two journalists had driven to Holmes's house in
their own car and Challes had followed. 'But it was
never my intention that they should be present at the
interview or the arrest of Holmes.' He agreed that when

156

Holmes came out of the house there had been a photographer there, and Holmes had 'expressed distress'.

John Scannell for Le Mesurier simply asked if his client was a man of previous good character. He was.

Sir David Napley then rose to his feet. Was Challes the senior supervisory officer concerned with the first Newton enquiry: 'And you conducted that enquiry into the Newton matter with all your usual skill and abilities?' 'Yes.' 'And on that occasion the charges in the present proceedings were not laid?' 'Yes.'

Sir David charted the relationship with Pencourt. Challes said he believed he first went to meet Penrose on 2 November 1977 at his home in Sanderstead, at the instigation of his Assistant Chief Constable at that time. He had spent between two or three hours with the journalists. Sir David was clearly determined to underline what he considered wrong police practice. He returned to the Bessell interviews in California. Why was it necessary for him to be introduced to Bessell by the journalists? 'Because Mr Bessell, in the presence of his attorneys, insisted or asked they should remain, and the attorneys agreed to this. I had no alternative but to agree, because if they did not remain I was not going to interview Bessell and my journey had been wasted.'

'Did you make any protest?' 'I indicated . . . I preferred not to have them there.'

When Sir David persisted, Challes said: 'I think one should say also that, at the interview which subsequently took place, there was no statement taken from Mr Bessell, and indeed this was not obtained until March, when Penrose and Courtiour were not present.' Sir David turned to Challes's preparation of Bessell's police statement for him from his *aide-memoire*. Showing indignation, and looking around at the press benches, he asked him if in his twenty six years of experience Challes had ever done anything like that before. The policeman replied that he had not. Smiling in polite exasperation, as Sir David repeatedly questioned him, he said it was the practice, in appropriate cases, for his force to prepare draft statements for witnesses but not from *aide-memoires*. This was simply because he had never had an *aide-memoire* before to work from. He thought it very unlikely that he would ever have one again.

Sir David switched subjects. What about Bessell's immunity? Challes said he had first known Bessell wanted immunity in August 1978, when he had had a call from the Director of Public Prosecutions' office. When Challes had first interviewed Bessell, he was worried about possible civil debts in this country. 'I could do nothing about civil matters, or about granting him immunity,' he said. He had mentioned Bessell's concern to his superiors and the Director's office, but did not think he had put it in writing.

Sir David wanted to know about alleged leaks of information. The last paragraph of Thorpe's second statement had in effect said that he had been advised not to answer any further questions because of the fear that there would be a leak. Was this a fair summary? 'Yes,' replied Challes. 'It was a very wise precaution, wasn't it?' 'Yes.' On 20 July 1978 – six weeks later – an article appeared in *Private Eye* called 'The Ditto Man'. Challes did not know who had leaked it. 'I have no idea but I am sure it did not come from me or anyone in my office.' He agreed that the previous December he had been concerned when Pencourt wrote a newspaper article on the interview he had conducted with Bessell. 'Did it shock you?' asked Sir David. Challes replied: 'There has been so much publication of articles about this case which concern me, I have gone beyond shock.'

Taylor's re-examination was brief. As far as Challes knew, no immunity had been granted to Miller. Bessell might have been worried about other things apart from civil debts, but no other matters had been mentioned specifically to Challes as 'being a matter of worry'.

Challes stepped off the stand on Thursday afternoon

and the prosecution evidence was over. So was the third week of the hearings, and although the original time-table had fallen to pieces, the hearings would enter a new, and final, phase on Monday morning when the lawyers started their submissions.

Everybody went home for a weekend's relaxation and preparation, spoilt only for a group of Special Branch officers at Heathrow, when they too were drag-ged into the case. After being told that a 'John Jeremy Thorpe' was intending to fly to San Francisco they rushed to the departure lounge to find a Leicester businessman with the same name as the former Liberal Leader innocently sipping a drink in the British Air-ways VIP departure lounge.

10

'The prosecution must have been desperate'

There was a slightly giggly, end-of-term atmosphere amongst the press as the fourth and final week began. Although the lawyers present knew the magistrates were unlikely to throw out such a big case, the defendants at last had their chance to hit back. Thorpe drifted in, wearing his charcoal-grey three-piece with the gold watch-chain, casually opening a letter. . . . Marion, cool and well-groomed as usual, wore her powder-grey cloak and large white beads, while Mrs Ursula Thorpe sat beside her in brown velvet jacket and silk scarf, flicking through *Woman's Weekly*.

George Deakin listened rather gloomily as his QC launched into a spirited hour-long attack on Andrew Newton. Now the Crown had fired all its guns, it was up to the four accused individually to persuade the magistrates that they had no case to answer. If any of them won, that was the end of it and they could walk away free – for good.

Gareth Williams went for Welsh rhetoric rather than legal precedents. Yes, Deakin had been in a conspiracy and admitted it. It had been an 'unsavoury agreement'. But it was not a conspiracy to murder: it was 'a conspiracy to frighten'. His client had been foolish in many ways, and he did not go as far as to ask for costs. Williams painted a picture of a little man, uninterested in politics, quite without powerful friends. 'He has been plucked from obscurity on the evidence of a single creature – Newton.'

'Newton was made and shaped by his own greed and self-delusion, finished and polished by the financial rewards he seeks.' Needing convictions to enable him to publish his memoirs, Newton's activities were 'an affront to the proper, ordered, course of justice . . . he has been paid, paid and paid again'. His testimony was uncorroborated and inconsistent. Thanks to Deakin's initiative in having reporting restrictions lifted, Newton and his accomplice Miller had conceded some of their wrong-doings, knowing they could be checked. To rely on Newton's evidence, Williams said, would be 'revolting'.

He then turned aside to make three complaints about 'important matters of principle'. First Chief Superintendent Challes had interviewed Bessell, a prime witness, in the presence of the journalists Penrose and Courtiour. In an ordinary case, such unique behaviour would be a scandal. Second came the immunities from prosecution. Newton had got one, and so to all intents and purposes had the Crown witness, Miller. Taylor conceded on behalf of the Crown that both, with others unknown, were regarded as co-conspirators. 'I criticize the quality of these people as witnesses.'

Finally, the magistrates had listened to a mass of sensational and salacious evidence which had very little to do with the charges. 'Every by-way and every irrelevancy in this case has been explored.' The charge against Deakin had nothing to do with currency dealings, bribery, or homosexuality.

Only Newton's evidence was there to implicate his client, sustained by an immunity and inducements from the press: 'Where a witness is so tainted and polluted by his own greed and participation, you should reject it,' Williams urged the Bench. Newton, with his sick mind, saw Deakin as 'a disposable human being', to be implicated as a link in the conspiracy. The gunman had perjured himself at his first trial; falsely testified Scott was a blackmailer; procured perjury in others; and had been promised enormous sums to bring about the conviction of Thorpe. Newton himself admitted he could not tell fact from fantasy: arriving in court on a serious matter, he turned up 'in a balaclava hat with eye-holes in it and curtains on the windows of his car'. Williams observed, heavily: 'He hasn't as yet, he says, had any psychiatric treatment.'

Williams plunged into detail. Deakin wanted someone to do something 'for a giggle', according to Miller. At the crucial Showman's dinner, Miller heard no talk about 'bumping off' and Newton himself was very drunk. Newton said there was a meeting at the Aust service station, but failed to say when, even to a month, and was vague. Deakin did not fit the description of one of the two men said to have stolen Scott's photograph. Newton claimed to have rung Deakin after shooting Rinka: Miller, although the Crown tried to press him, merely described a conversation consistent with a 'frightener'.

'Mr Deakin should not be dragged down with the others.' Newton himself said he was merely bungling a murder attempt to try and frighten Scott. The £5000 pay-off was not alleged to have come from Deakin. Miller taped Deakin saying: '"Yeah, well, I'm denying,"' but this did not show what he was denying, or whether it was true. Miller's taping indicated 'the amount of sanctimonious humbug in this court'. Witnesses all said they were acting out of public duty 'which happens to be greased along the way by large sums of money from the press'.

'It is not my part to pass any comment about the conduct of anyone in this case: someone will have to consider how far the press can go or be allowed to go in matters which could be the subject of criminal investigation. In some ways at least they have performed a useful public function. In some ways, their conduct has not been free from blemish.' He added, comparatively light-heartedly: 'Or even a wart or nodule.'

Williams's submission wound up with an appeal to 'the fair-minded scrutiny of an independent magistracy'.

George Deakin was entitled to return to his obscurity, he said.

Peter Taylor got to his feet for the Crown's right of reply. He pointed out dryly what the law was. According to Lord Parker's 'practice direction' of 1962, there were only two grounds for refusing to commit. The first was when there was no evidence to prove an essential element in the charge. The second was when evidence was so discredited by cross-examination or so manifestly unreliable 'that no reasonable tribunal could safely convict on it'. The magistrates could not throw the case out because they themselves would not convict: if a reasonable tribunal *might* convict, then there was a case to answer.

Deakin had admitted he was party to an unlawful conspiracy. There was clear evidence Newton had been commissioned to do something. 'You don't get offered £15,000 or £10,000 or even £5000 to go and *frighten* someone.' All that mattered about the airport phone call to Deakin was whether it was made at all: 'If Deakin had dropped out, there was no point in ringing him.'

The notable informer Maurice O'Mahoney had once implicated 150 people in a great series of burglaries and robberies. It had been ruled then that a jury, provided the trial judge warned them of the dangers, could go ahead and convict on the uncorroborated evidence of an accomplice. But the Crown had other evidence to throw in the scales. Miller's tapes showed Deakin helping arrange contact with the jailed Newton, and knowing about the final pay-off. Of the phrase 'I'm denying,' Taylor observed: '*Qui s'excuse, s'accuse.*' Newton did not actually *need* to implicate Deakin, although his profits from the press might have been in bad taste: 'The question is whether the story is true, not how many people he sold it to.'

Williams, as the defence, was allowed a final word in accordance with court procedure. Taylor had mentioned Newton's 'chequered history'. Williams said sarcastically: 'Chequebook history!' If Taylor was so unyielding,

'Committal proceedings are a farce, and the magistracy no more than a pliant instrument to commit people for trial.'

Sir David Napley's hour had at last come round. He stood up knowing his client's alleged misdeeds had received remorseless publicity, with blaring headlines day after day from Sydney to San Francisco. The defence version of events would never be heard in these preliminary proceedings. He could not call his defence witnesses, or his client himself into the witness box, until the trial if it took place. But what he could do was make as powerful a legal case as possible that the three local justices should not commit Thorpe for trial before a judge and jury. To do this, he had to show that the Crown evidence, with its thirty-eight witnesses (twenty-eight written and ten in person), 128 exhibits, statements, pictures and tape-recordings, was legally worthless.

'I'm bound to call heavily on your patience,' he told the JPs, who were to listen stoically for three hours. 'The eyes of the world are on the court.' Britons were now discussing whether committal proceedings should be abolished, or closed to the press. Sir David did not take those views, he said. 'The purpose of committal proceedings is not merely to provide a rubber stamp for the prosecution. . . . They provide the last safeguard between the citizen and the higher court.' Sir David warned he would go into highly complex areas of conspiracy law: nonetheless, he did not want the magistrates to shrug off the issue to the judges.

Much of Sir David's argument centred around Bessell, the former Liberal MP. He, as prime witness, had given a vast amount of evidence which was inadmissible. Furthermore he was 'utterly unreliable' and a liar.

Sir David made a dramatic claim about the conspiracy charge, which ran from 1 October 1968 to 1 November 1977, 'a longer period than it takes an elephant to gestate its young'. He had discussed it with Holmes's counsel, John Mathew, who was 'the most able prosecutor this country has ever known', and a senior treasury counsel. Some matters in the case were 'virtually unique, I repeat unique, in the administration of criminal law in this country'. Judges had warned of the danger of marathon conspiracy counts of more than five years. Mathew's view confirmed his own experience 'that there has never been in the history of this country a conspiracy charge alleged over a period of nine years'. 'You may ask yourself why the prosecution has embarked upon that sort of charge . . . it is an attempt to introduce into this case evidence which, if the conspiracy had been charged as it should have been, would not have been admissible – and is not admissible.'

Why was Thorpe alone charged with incitement? It was because it was a 'fail-safe exercise'. 'It is a long stop; because if that fails, they hope to come home by some means on a second charge. That, in my submission, is the reason why Mr Thorpe stands charged on these two matters.'

Over the period of nine years there had been alleged 'a series of separate and wholly unconnected incidents'. 'The evidence of these earlier matters is not admissible in proof of the ultimate alleged conspiracy in February 1975.' The case did not stand if other, different conspiracies came into the picture. But anyway, Sir David further argued, there had been no earlier conspiracies at all. And the essential thing about the law of conspiracy was that there had to be agreement from first to last. 'You must have before you that at some stage in this evidence there was an agreement by which two or more parties bound themselves to a particular plan or concept, and it is against this background that I shall invite you to say that the prosecution has not made out its case.'

(Sir David reminded the magistrates in passing that statements made to the police by other defendants were not admissible against Thorpe, nor were statements on the tapes. 'They are not, any of them, in furtherance of the conspiracy. They are all *ex-post facto*.')

Sir David explained he was going to examine first the

direct evidence. 'I contend that in terms of direct evidence the case for the prosecution stands or falls on the evidence of Mr Bessell.' 'Incident One', as he described it, was before Christmas 1968. Only Bessell and Thorpe were present. They were supposedly talking about ways to dispose of Scott. Bessell had said in his deposition: '"At no time did I consider that I was bound by an agreement to join in any plan to murder Norman Scott."' Nor was Holmes ever bound. 'There was clearly not a conspiracy there, because a man in law cannot conspire with himself. That is the end of Incident One.'

Similarly, no one had been bound by agreement during Incident Two – a three-way discussion between Thorpe, Bessell and Holmes of murder methods. This was Bessell's testimony in the witness box.

Incident Three was the 'American charade' to placate Thorpe. Play-acting did not amount to conspiracy. This only left Incident Four, the Showman's dinner in Blackpool in February 1975. For the first time, it was said, there was a specific plan – to have Newton kill Scott. But it was in January 1974 that Bessell had done his 'so-called disappearing act': he had gone to America over a year earlier. 'He says: "I heard no more of the Scott affair between January 1974 and Christmas 1975," when, he says, Holmes telephoned him.'

There was not a shred or a tittle of evidence 'to connect Mr Thorpe with what occurred immediately before, on, or after the Showman's dinner, by way of direct evidence'. What Holmes supposedly said later was not admissible against Thorpe.

The first three incidents could not be used in evidence in proof of Incident Number Four. 'The Crown case is that Incident Four was a specific plan between Holmes, Le Mesurier, Miller and Deakin to employ Newton to shoot Scott. This is the *gravamen* that they are making; not some fanciful discussion of the type described by Mr Bessell. What they are alleging is that a plan was made, an integral part of which was Mr Newton and his conduct, to shoot Mr Scott. And that was the whole beginning and end of the conspiracy. Quite clearly prior to February 1975, there is not, again, a scintilla of evidence to show that Mr Thorpe, Mr Bessell or Mr Holmes had ever discussed that type, or that actual plan. There is no evidence of it at all. Search as you will, it is not there. There is no suggestion that Mr Bessell played any part in it. There is no evidence that Mr Thorpe took any part in it, either in formulating a plan, or working out details, or in doing anything more.'

The ultimate plan was 'a completely new concept on the basis that the prosecution put it'. If, then, the prosecution were unable to produce any direct evidence, they might perforce have to scrape the barrel and try to find some other way of bringing in matters from which they could infer that Thorpe was a party to a crime, or conspiracy.

How might they do that? They might say there was evidence that Thorpe secured a payment of two sums of £10,000 through Hayward; that he caused it to be paid 'by a devious route' into Dinshaw's Jersey account; that he released the money to Holmes; and that he induced Bessell to write a letter to Barnes – 'although there is not evidence to support it' – for the purposes of the Newton trial. There was an alleged phone conversation in which it was said: 'David should "take the ferry".' The Crown might say it could be inferred from this that Thorpe was party and privy to the conspiracy. They might also say that Thorpe tried to pressurize Bessell through Hayward to stop him coming back to England; and that he put pressure on Dinshaw concerning the £10,000.

The Crown also might say there was an inference to be drawn from the one payment of £10,000 – that it was for the £2500 paid for the letters. That would be 'grossly misleading to the court'. There was no evidence Thorpe knew of the purchase of the letters. He had told police he had '"no knowledge whatsoever"' of it.

The prosecution sought to relate the second £10,000 payment received in November 1975 to the payment to Newton of £5000 on 18 April 1977. Why, if Holmes had to pay £5000 to Newton, did he need more money? He already had £7500 in hand, Sir David stressed. And again, Thorpe had asked for a total of £17,000 in November 1974. The conspirators were supposed to have got the money together against the possibility of finding someone for the plan. This was 'wandering with Alice in Wonderland'. No reasonable jury would accept it for one moment. The amounts and dates did not tally. It was 'the last desperate act of the prosecution'.

Sir David then read from one of Mr Thorpe's letters from the House of Commons to Hayward in July 1975. It asked for money but said there was '"no urgency"'. 'There is no evidence at all that the payment of £5000 ever came from the Hayward money. There is not a trace of evidence.'

Sir David returned again to the Barnes letter which Bessell had said he was persuaded to write. How could a letter requested in January 1976 be evidence of an alleged conspiracy to murder in 1975? 'It does not begin to touch the essential.'

It was 'palpable nonsense' to suggest that the letters said to have been bought by Holmes for £2500 might fall into the hands of the police. At the time, the letters were known to a string of people including the Home Secretary.

It was alleged Thorpe had tried to pressurize Bessell and Dinshaw. These allegations were not evidence indicating his taking part in a conspiracy. He had made it plain he was in no way involved in the alleged conspiracy to murder, but said he was concerned about the political implications. It might be said that Jeremy Thorpe had failed to exercise proper control of the money entrusted to him by Hayward, but not that he had paid it for any nefarious purpose.

As for Scott, 'the vast bulk of Scott's evidence in this case has as much to do with the case as the flowers that bloom in the spring. The truth of the matter is that, at the end of the day, I wholly concede you do not have to worry very much about the main issue presented by Mr

Scott; whether there was a homosexual relationship as he alleges with Mr Thorpe, or not, as Mr Thorpe asserts.'

Sir David went on: 'Whether or not there was, I would concede the mere fact that a man was making these allegations made sufficient nuisance for someone, of the nature and mind, to want to get rid of him.'

Scott had clearly accepted in evidence that 'many of the stories he told were lies he had told over many years'. Sir David now proposed to catalogue them 'to see the sort of man with whom we are dealing'. Scott claimed two policemen took letters from him and then denied having them; he claimed to have had a homosexual relationship with a Mr Lowrey; he said the solicitor Ross refused to mention Thorpe in his divorce proceedings; he made allegations against Van der Vater; and, 'not for the first time', against his own mother; he alleged he had had an intimate relationship with a Mrs Weight and said Mr Weight turned him out because he was a 'cuckolded husband'; he had said David Ennals, a Minister of the Crown, was involved in 'disgusting conduct'; he had accused Sir David himself of belonging to the 'cover-up'; and accused Ron Mount, of the *News of the World*, of writing an article about him before they had even met.

Sir David paused and leant forward: 'Mention a name to Mr Scott and he will make allegations,' he said, heavily.

Scott had also said he had told Jimmy Collier of his homosexual relationship with Thorpe. But Collier, in evidence, said that he never had such a discussion. Mrs Collier, according to Scott, had discussed a quarrel he had had with Thorpe. But Mrs Collier said that was untrue. Scott had also said he told Mrs Collier at the hotel that he was going to kill himself and Thorpe. She wholly denied this. 'That is some fair indication of the value you can place on that man's evidence when the opportunity comes to test it.'

Scott maintained he had only talked about the alleged relationship because of the Insurance cards. But he had held an Insurance card in April 1962 and had had no real grievance. 'He has been mentally unbalanced for the whole of his life . . . he says now he has been better for the last three years. You saw him in the witness box, you saw the outbursts that occurred. You can form your own judgement from his demeanour about that.'

Scott had offered to show the court the word 'incurable' cut into his arm. 'What sort of mental state do you think Mr Scott has? He has told a series of lies and long stories which in my submission although he does not accept it, amounts to fantasy. His Insurance cards, in my submission, have become an obsession, an obsession which has centred on Mr Thorpe.'

Sir David then produced the strangest analogy of the hearing. If Taylor, instead of conducting the magistrates through the case, had taken them to a mental institution, and produced a man who said he was the King of Siam and that he had had a homosexual relationship with the Kaiser, and then said to him: 'Are you telling the truth now?' what sort of answer would they get?

The mind was a delicate instrument. People with obsessions were difficult people to deal with. They convinced themselves of the truth of their stories. 'That is the picture I present to you of Mr Scott.' Only two letters had been produced from Thorpe, which clearly were not love letters. The Crown might try to make something of 'Bunnies' and a postscript saying: '"I miss you."' 'You have to have a pretty salacious mind to read that into a letter to a man with a mental condition.' What possible reason could Thorpe have for wanting Scott killed in February 1975 when he had had no contact with him since July 1965? A long list of people had known fully of Scott's allegations. They included Liberal Party colleagues, newspapers, and there had been the outburst at the inquest of Mrs Parry-Jones. Thorpe had told the police that 'the worst that Scott could falsely allege had been revealed'.

The evidence on Incidents One, Two and Three was inadmissible and there was no evidence in law of Thorpe having engaged in conspiracy. The incitement charge related to an alleged nine-year-old incident. Bessell did not believe he was being invited to arrange anyone's death. 'The prosecution has to be pretty hard pressed to rely on this charge.' 'This clearly and manifestly stands or falls on the evidence of Bessell.' There was no evidence to show inducements or persuasion or threats were held out. 'The Crown has not got even remotely a chance of it being proved.'

'Can you imagine there could ever have been a prosecution in this or any other country where the three principal witnesses unconditionally accept, apart from the evidence in this case, they have always been inveterate liars?' Sir David only proposed to deal with Bessell because the case stood or fell on him. No jury would accept him as being a reliable witness. Bessell had been given a wide immunity – the danger of these had been 'roundly condemned' by Lord Justice Lawton. The prosecution 'must have been desperate' to give Bessell such a wide-ranging immunity of which nobody, in his experience, had seen the like.

It must have been made crystal-clear to Bessell and his lawyers that they would 'have to come up with something good' or he would not get the immunity. He had even been given immunity by the Director of Public Prosecutions against prosecution by a private person, which was quite wrong. 'It is a precedent which ought not to be followed again and, in my submission, ought to disqualify him.'

Sir David paused and re-arranged his papers. He looked up. 'Chequebook journalism,' he said. He thought it a fair assessment that something like £250,000 had already changed hands to various people involved in books, interviews and articles. It was reasonable that if there were convictions this could rise to half a million pounds. 'Some of the witnesses actually committed themselves to articles and books while in the witness box,' he said. Bessell had had payment on account of £50,000 from the *Sunday Telegraph*. If Thorpe was acquitted it would be exceedingly difficult to serialize anything because of the libel laws. 'You have got to ask if this is not a considerable inducement if you consider Bessell's impecunious position.' How could there be a fair trial, with such inducements?

There was another subject which was linked – 'Orchestration'. At every turn one found Penrose and Courtiour interviewing witnesses on the conditions where they were clearly anxious to make – as they did – very considerable sums of money. Most particularly they had had contact with Bessell. They had spent six days with him. They had discussed theories and argued. 'They were trying to piece something together to make it presentable,' was the implication of the meetings.

'There may be a case sometimes for investigative journalism but it does not mean you can ever lose sight of the dangers of it, particularly when it is linked to money of the amounts involved in this case.'

It had been agreed that Bessell's evidence in court was very similar in phraseology to that of his *aide-memoire*. 'This shows first of all it came out of the *aide-memoire* and secondly shows he learnt it by heart.' Challes said he had been given extracts from the *aide-memoire* to prepare a draft statement. He had done an 'unwise and an undesirable thing'.

'Can you think of anything worse than someone giving evidence from a statement drafted by the police officer conducting this case? He [Challes] would not answer my question directly as to whether he would ever do it again. One suspects we know his answer.' Bessell had been put in touch with Scott after many years by Penrose and Courtiour at 'the beginning of what I termed the Orchestration in this matter'. Bessell had been unwilling to see Challes and give his account. He had decided to tell the truth after being a liar for many years but he would not speak unless Penrose and Courtiour were present. 'Does not that strike you as being dangerous and making his evidence unreliable?'

He reminded the Bench that Thorpe on his advice had not answered questions. One of the reasons was 'because of the Orchestration and leakage that had gone on'. It had proved to be very wise.

The magistrates were showing clear signs of strain by this stage. Donati was blinking rapidly and chewing his pencil as he struggled to keep his notes up with Sir David's many points. Sir David looked up at them. They had got to assess what they had thought of Bessell in the witness box. 'In my submission, when you looked at his demeanour, mendacity was oozing out of every pore of his body.' Pencourt had fabricated a letter to try to bring a link between Newton and Holmes. The letter in law, was a forgery. When the case was over, it could well be a matter which would be investigated. 'It is quite clear that large financial motives were attracting Bessell. . . . It is not enough to say Bessell made allegations against Mr Thorpe, and therefore, "Let the jury decide."' Bessell had deceived his creditors and had attempted a '$1-million fraud' on Hayward. 'He clearly accepts he was a party to it, but, as crafty as one would expect him to be, he turned it on me by saying: "Your client was a party to it." Do you not think this was a carefully rehearsed answer?' It was a false one, Sir David said. Bessell had written letters acknowledging he was solely responsible. The sort of man who would support two different people at once for the leadership of the Liberal Party, he was an experienced speaker and lay preacher, as well as a former MP. It was quite evident Bessell had rehearsed what he was going to say.

'He accepts Mr Thorpe was contemplating murder but concedes he did nothing about it. Yet he was content to leave him as Leader of the Party. Should he not have gone at pretty good speed to a psychiatrist?'

Bessell had accepted he had a 'credulity problem' [in the evidence this had been given as a 'credibility' problem]. 'There is no reasonably minded jury who would begin to accept the evidence of someone of that background, who gave his evidence in the tailored way in which Mr Bessell has given his.' His evidence was 'utterly discredited'.

Sir David turned from Bessell to his own client. 'I do not ask for any special treatment of Mr Thorpe. It would be grossly improper. But I do ask that because he is Mr Thorpe he should not be treated any worse.' Sir David invited the Bench: 'Forget, as it were, the names of the defendants, and regard them as people who might be called Passmore, Blackmore, Westcott, and Venn – all good Somerset names.'

If they were dealing with four ordinary people and had heard the enormities he had related, would they entertain the case for one moment?

He gave Taylor notice now, that if he attempted to deal with the facts in his reply, rather than the law: 'I shall be on my feet every time.'

It was not proper to have brought the case. It was not only unreliable but it was not possible to conduct a case fairly against the background. Sir David wholly conceded that it was not the magistrates' function to try the case. But he did submit, in deciding whether or not there was a *prima facie* case, that in reaching their decision they were just as obliged to give the benefit of the doubt as in any other case. 'If you are going to send Mr Thorpe for trial with all that it involves in terms of cost, anxiety and publicity, you have got to satisfy yourself there has been made out a case upon which a reasonably minded jury would be likely to convict. In my submission the prosecution has failed in every step to make that out in the case of Mr Thorpe.'

It was 4 p.m. There would obviously be no more defence submissions that day. But Taylor was immediately on his feet. With respect, he wished to point out to the magistrates, Sir David had referred to those prosecuting as having salacious minds and being desperate. 'In a number of respects I submit he has selected the evidence in a way which would be misleading and I wish to correct.' Taylor said he could have done it by 'jumping up and down' but he had chosen not to. He sat down.

Sir David jumped up, and explained at great length how he had not been referring to the prosecution lawyers, 'his learned friends', personally.

That evening, Minehead's temporary press corps threw a party in the Wellington Hotel. Ribald songs ('If you come to Minehead/Be sure to watch your arse . . .') about the proceedings were made up and sung. The reporters each paid £5 for food and drink for their guests – telephonists and friends they had made in their hotels – and the celebrations went on until the early hours. Deakin and Le Mesurier were invited and made an appearance.

11

A case to answer

Peter Taylor was in a brisk mood when the court reconvened in the morning. He got straight down to business. 'I would like to make it absolutely clear what the prosecution case is, and how it is put,' he said. 'There are two charges and they are not in any way meant to overlap or be alternatives, or, to use any of Sir David's phrases, "long stops, fall backs, fail safes" or anything of that kind; they are quite separate.' The first charge was incitement. The Crown's case was that on a day early in 1969 at the House of Commons Thorpe incited Holmes to murder Scott. The second charge was one of conspiracy in which Thorpe was charged jointly with the other accused.

'Sir David seems to have been under the misapprehension that the Crown was suggesting a series of conspiracies in January 1969 and later dates when Thorpe, on the evidence, suggested killing Mr Scott from time to time. Sir David based a great deal of his argument on the assertions that there were a number of separate conspiracies, not one, that they should have been charged separately, and that the evidence of one was not evidence in relation to the other. All of that, with the greatest respect to Sir David, is completely beside the point. The prosecution's case is that there was one conspiracy and one conspiracy only and that it came into existence after a number of attempts by Thorpe over a number of years to persuade someone to join him, someone who finally did, to kill Scott.

'As soon as somebody else agreed, there was a conspiracy. The case for the Crown is that Thorpe from 1968-9 onwards was urging there should be agreement to kill Scott, but nobody agreed with him until some time when Holmes did agree.' It was not suggested the conspiracy came into existence in October 1968. 'It was probably about 1974 when Holmes was converted to the view that Thorpe was right and that he then agreed with Thorpe, and it was then there was a conspiracy.' The prosecution might narrow the indictment at trial to read '1973-7' instead of '1968-77', but the dates were not, as Sir David had suggested, any sort of device to get in evidence which was inadmissible. 'If the charge was 1973-7, the evidence would still have been admissible.'

Sir David had said the eyes of the world were on Minehead. 'I am not going to say anything in this case about that, and I am not going to go into sweeping generalizations about English legal history,' Taylor said, acidly, 'but if anybody does do that, it is important to check the facts and, with the greatest respect to Sir David, when he talked of there being no previous example in English law of a case in which a conspiracy was alleged over a five-year period, he failed to check his facts, even in relation to his own office.' Sir David looked up sharply.

Taylor remarked that he was not as experienced as Sir David, but in the last five years he had had personal experience of three cases. The first was Poulson and Pottinger in 1973 – a seven-year conspiracy; the second Poulson, Dan Smith and Andrew Cunningham in 1974 – eight years; and there was a third – McCulloch and others at Teesside in January 1976, where the conspiracy lasted over fourteen years. 'Sir David Napley's firm represented one of the defendants in that case,' he said. (There was laughter from the press benches.) 'The assertion blazed over the press that the charge is without precedent is wholly unfounded.'

Taylor's next topic was startling – the Crown Jewels. But it was only an analogy. Say somebody tried to do something outrageous, like trying to steal the Crown

Jewels. If it was the idea of A, it might take a considerable period of time before he could get B to join him but if B did join him, the whole 'history of persuasion' would be wholly admissible evidence. It did not matter if the conspiracy got down through C and D to E, who then got cold feet, and A had stayed in the background and arranged to procure the money. If he had procured the money to pay E 'of course he is a member of the conspiracy'.

From 1968 onwards, Thorpe had been trying from time to time to persuade those who came into contact with him closely that 'the ultimate solution' ought to be put into operation. 'So all the evidence of the preceding period when Thorpe was urging this from time to time becomes material.'

The evidence of motive goes back even further, to 1961. 'It may be an unusual situation to be looking so far back, but this is a very unusual case, a quite exceptional case, some have said a unique case, but the principle is not different.'

Having laid the general groundwork, Taylor then turned to what he called 'corrections on matters of fact' – some errors, some significant omissions. Sir David had said the previous day, when talking about the incitement charge, there was no evidence that it went any further than a discussion. It was absolutely essential that the court was reminded what the evidence was. Bessell had been specifically cross-examined by Sir David on the basis that all that had taken place at the Commons was a discussion. He had rejected that flatly. (Sir David, sitting beside Taylor, adjusted his glasses and started leafing through the depositions.) Bessell had said it was raised as 'a serious proposal' and one for which Holmes had been invited specifically to London.

'The person who does the inciting is the criminal.' It was not important whether Bessell took it seriously or not.

Then there was the 'Isaac Foot' answer. Thorpe used it in a telephone conversation with Bessell, who had told

Thorpe he must know the truth. He had said: '"So the plan David told me about was real." Mr Thorpe said: "Yes." I said: "Thank God it failed so it can never be tried again." Thorpe said: "No, that's right it cannot be tried again."' That, said Taylor, was 'testimony a reasonable jury properly directed might infer was an admission by Mr Thorpe that he was fully part and parcel of a plan which failed'.

Sir David had also made 'a vital omission' when referring to the money from Hayward. When Thorpe had been talking to Dinshaw comparatively recently he referred specifically to the fact he had loaned £5000 to Holmes 'who needed it very badly'. 'If that is included it hobbles and scotches all of Sir David's arguments.'

Having cleaned up those points, Taylor went back to the two charges. The words used in the Act to define incitement were very significant: '"Whosoever shall solicit, encourage, persuade or endeavour to persuade or shall propose to any person to murder any other person. . . ."' Thorpe's proposal to Holmes had been a serious one, and various suggestions had been made about how it should be done including a gun, poison, and then a slow-working poison. 'Unless Bessell can be regarded as a witness wholly discredited, there is a case.' There was the matter of immunity which Sir David had raised. What was the inducement being offered to Bessell by giving him immunity? 'There was no question of him being prosecuted. He did not need to have the immunity. He could have stayed put where he was.' The evidence was that Bessell had not asked for immunity but his solicitors had.

Taylor made a legal joke by saying that 'Solicitors are always prudent,' and Thorpe laughed out loud as he sat on his bench. It was absurd to suggest that a grant of immunity invalidated someone's evidence, and it had never been the intention of the DPP to give Bessell immunity from perjury. He could be extradited from California if he committed it. 'I submit a red herring was raised in the Divisional Court and here.' Bessell had

179

been severely attacked by Sir David, but again and again contemporary documents tended to confirm what he said.

On the conspiracy charge the 'Isaac Foot' answer was, Taylor submitted, 'direct evidence of admittance by Thorpe he was involved in an abortive attempt to kill Scott that had failed and could not be tried again. If that is correct it is a case on its own.' There was abundant evidence of motive. Again, Sir David had many criticisms of Scott but his evidence over the years was supported by documents. Thorpe had done things to keep Scott at bay such as paying the solicitor's fees, the retainer, and for the Swiss trip.

Then there was a 'wholly untainted source' – the money and the evidence of Hayward and Dinshaw. 'When one looks at Thorpe's statement, the Crown submit that it is telling three lies.' Firstly it was untrue that the avoidance of paying money into the Party funds had anything to do with Hayward. Secondly, it was untrue that the £20,000 in two lots of £10,000 had been deposited with accountants, and thirdly it was untrue it was being held as an 'iron reserve' against shortage of funds in a subsequent election. 'If that were right it would still be there. We haven't had another election.'

When matters were warming up, Thorpe tried to get Dinshaw to tell lies about the money, then made 'a crude and silly threat' when Dinshaw refused.

'There is evidence of Mr Thorpe,' Taylor said gravely, and pausing slightly, added: ' – I am sorry to have to say this – trying to interfere with the course of justice. On 4 April 1978, he sought to persuade Hayward to put pressure on Bessell to prevent his coming here, although it was said in the Divisional Court that Mr Thorpe would welcome his evidence.' It was a rather nasty threat that if carried out would have meant that Bessell could not go back to America to marry the lady he was living with. 'The second instance was attempts to persuade Dinshaw to tell lies and, when he wouldn't, a kind of muffled threat. This is evidence of the lengths to which Mr

Thorpe was prepared to go when finding himself in a difficult situation.'

Taylor sat down, and Sir David immediately rose beside him to reply. Leaning back with his arms behind him and resting on the bench, he said that one thing was crystal clear. What he was saying was that the earlier meetings had not been conspiracies at all, because there was no agreement between people. The charge was not comparable to the Poulson cases; because it described a conspiracy on 'divers days'. If the conspiracy alleged by the Crown only related to 1975-7 Bessell could not help at all. He had departed the country in January 1974. Sir David entirely accepted Taylor's correction about the McCulloch case which his firm had been involved in. But he had been away from the office for a month and there was difficulty in getting reference books. (Taylor theatrically turned his head to stare at the large pile of reference books which had been amassed behind Sir David.) Sir David repeated there was no evidence of persuasion on the incitement charge. 'At the very most it is a proposal, a discussion.' Taylor had also said Sir David had omitted the reference to Holmes getting £5000 because he was hard up. If Taylor was now saying money was needed badly this was quite inconsistent with the letter Thorpe sent to Hayward, saying there was no urgency. It was possible there had been a conspiracy to frighten by some people. But the magistrates must not draw inference on speculation. Even if there was around 1975 some sort of conspiracy, what evidence was there that at that time Thorpe was a party to it, or knew of it? 'No case has been made out on either count against Mr Thorpe for trial on this matter,' he concluded.

Now it was the turn of John Mathew for Holmes. He chose a different tack. Quite insufficient evidence existed, he submitted, for a conspiracy to kill, as distinct from a conspiracy to do anything else. That, after all, was the charge against his client.

He told the magistrates, who were visibly tiring under the weight of words, that he would be short. He wanted to examine the case 'quietly and realistically, without emotive criticism and arguments better put before a jury'. But first he had something to say about the evidence. There *was* some against Holmes, of course. If there was not he would never have been charged. 'But I do submit,' he said, looking the chairman straight in the eye, 'the quality of the evidence, given against a background of intrigue, rumour and self-interest probably without parallel, has been shown to be the most corrupt and tainted ever to be placed before a court of criminal jurisdiction.'

The press wrote his categoric statement for their headlines, and Mathew turned to hard facts. He made an immediate concession. He would not accept for one moment that it had been proved there was an arrangement to frighten Scott, as opposed to killing him, but he would concede there was sufficient evidence on this for the consideration of a higher court.

'Once you accept there is some evidence of a conspiracy of a lesser nature, the great bulk of the Crown evidence falls into place, and is explained as being in accordance with that, rather than a conspiracy to commit the ultimate offence.' He emphasized his point with chopping motions of the first two fingers of his left hand. What did it matter if Holmes might have tried to get documents from a briefcase? If he had arranged for Scott to go to a hotel in Bristol? If he had met and talked to Newton? If he had tried to get a letter from Bessell? 'All these facts add nothing to the Crown's case that there was a conspiracy to murder. There may be a *prima facie* case for conspiracy, but not conspiracy to murder.'

The evidence against Holmes on this point came down to only a couple of pages of Bessell's deposition, half a page of Newton, and one line out of all the tapes. There was the meeting between Newton and Holmes at the Royal Court Hotel. Newton had said his brief was to kill Scott and he had been told it was preferable Scott should vanish off the face of the earth. 'This is the only part of Newton's evidence which tends to show something more

182

than a conspiracy to frighten.' But was Newton's evidence reliable? Mathew said pointedly that he would not refer to other cases involving 'great criminal turn-coats' because it did not really help. It was normal for a jury to consider evidence – unless the committing tribunal came to the conclusion that it was so 'manifestly unreliable' that no jury could really ever accept it. On this point, he would merely adopt what Williams had said about Newton. Just to rub it in, he then called him a liar, a perjuror, a man who had no regard for justice and had admitted his greed and dishonesty. Newton had made allegations of blackmail against Scott in a statement to the police, in great circumstantial detail – 'a total figment of his imagination'. 'He has made money, is making money and is going to continue to make money if there are convictions. . . . Can there be a more discredited witness? Is it possible to imagine any circumstances which would make a witness more manifestly unreliable? It is evidence on which you cannot rely.'

Next came the tape-recording of the conversation between Newton and Holmes. Newton needed extra evidence to complete his package for the newspapers, so he had called at Holmes's house to provoke Holmes into telephoning him. This phone-call was in October 1977: at the end of a conversation lasting ten minutes, there was nothing about a conspiracy to kill except Newton saying: 'Don't forget there is a charge that can be put on to us, a conspiracy to bloody murder.' This was at a time when everybody had been alerted to what Bessell was saying and, of course, a conspiracy to murder charge was a possibility. There was a police inquiry going on. 'This part of the evidence,' Mathew said firmly, 'is of no value because of the circumstances.'

Finally, there was the evidence of Bessell. What he said was that on the way to the airport to California Holmes had 'quite gratuitously indicated the truth of the matter – that he [Holmes] had been party to an arrangement by which Scott should be shot'.

'If you decide to disregard Mr Newton's evidence and

are then left with Mr Bessell and nothing else, standing on its own it is quite insufficient. Without Mr Newton this prosecution would never have been brought at all. If one stands back and considers the whole of this case without Mr Newton, if one erases the whole of his evidence, in my submission such a gaping void could never be filled by this minimal piece of evidence from such a dubious character as Mr Bessell. Does not Mr Bessell fall into the same bracket of discredited witness?'

Now Mathew turned his sights on Bessell. He had admitted lying in the past; being party to a 'one-million-dollar fraud' on Hayward; he was 'on the golden bandwagon of payment from the media'; he had disappeared in dubious circumstances in 1974. 'Whatever Mr Bessell might say was his wish, he received that very wide-ranging immunity. Whether that was in the public interest has nothing to do with this court. But who doubts he would ever have been in the witness box without it?' Bessell had been quite happy to continue his friendship and support for Thorpe despite what he said had happened in 1969 and 1970. He said he was told about the murder plan by Holmes in January 1976. 'But his "holier than thou attitude" did not come upon him until a very great deal later.' If he had been told, he had played along until the 'golden carrot' had been dangled in telephone calls from Penrose and Courtiour.

Referring back to Sir David's submission, Mathew said it was being suggested that Penrose and Courtiour had 'orchestrated' the allegation. It was not necessary to adopt that attitude, but what was relevant about the whole matter was that they were in the background all the time. They had been present at Bessell's *insistence*. All this made Bessell's evidence quite valueless.

In summary, he said, returning to his main theme after half an hour, there was evidence of conspiracy not to kill, but to frighten. The magistrates should not forget that the Scott threat was much greater in 1969 than in 1975. Newton had maintained that he wanted not to shoot, but to frighten, Scott. And then there was Miller, 'nominated at the twelfth hour – not even the eleventh – as a conspirator by the Crown'. Miller himself had indicated that it went no further than a conspiracy to frighten.

Mathew paused slightly and dropped his voice. 'This saga has been exaggerated out of all proportion to the true facts,' he said, his voice rising steadily, 'by witnesses with unbalanced minds, or with the most dangerous motives, or both. Perhaps when the good names of public figures are put in jeopardy by rumour and speculation masquerading as fact, perhaps it is necessary the facts should be laid bare for public scrutiny. The value of this evidence has been publicly and fully examined. No one can say that has not been done. No one can any longer be accused of any covering-up. The time has now come in my submission to ring the curtain down.'

Taylor was on his feet immediately. It would be quite wrong for the Bench to accede to any blandishments about it being necessary to air the matter and then put it away. The question was quite simply whether there was a case on which Holmes should face trial. Mathew had accepted there was *prima facie* evidence a payment had been made to Newton, that there were arrangements between Holmes and Newton, and here was 'a possible *prima facie* case of arrangement to frighten Scott'. Therefore he was accepting the *prima facie* cogency of a good deal of evidence in the case. 'But then he seeks to chop off the conspiracy to kill. This is an inconsistent stand to adopt.'

He admitted, Taylor said, that if Newton 'might' be telling the truth the whole submission fell to the ground. Mathew interjected: 'I agree.' But on the tape-recorded conversation 'murder' had been specifically referred to. Nobody would admit to having done something if they had not done it. Taylor added – leafing through his transcript and then looking up at the magistrates – that it was Holmes who introduced the word 'conspiracy', and then did not show surprise at the words 'conspiracy to murder'. Bessell's evidence was of a clear admission by Holmes in a taxi in California that Newton was hired to kill Scott, that Holmes had found him through friends, and that he was being enriched to the extent of £5000.

Mathew had not referred to the money agreed to be paid or being paid. If the evidence was credible, it was agreed to pay £10,000 and 'after the debacle' £5000 was paid. It must be open to any reasonable jury to think that was the sort of sum consistent with a conspiracy to kill, not to frighten. Taylor concluded briskly: 'It is not sufficient to pick off bits of the evidence. It's the totality.'

Mathew, rising slowly, said he did not disagree. But nothing could corroborate Newton if he was incapable of belief. If he was capable of belief, then there was a *prima facie* case which would be hotly disputed at the trial. If he was not, and Newton therefore went out, they were left with Bessell. 'I am putting everything on the dismissal of Mr Newton.'

He also had a short word about the £10,000. There was no evidence this was the original figure, except from the mouth of Newton. Taylor was appearing to agree that £5000 must have meant more than a conspiracy to frighten. But Newton had spent two years in jail. 'The fact that it was only £5000 in the circumstances of this case would clearly indicate it was not a conspiracy to murder,' he said.

Taylor, who by this time was turning round to glance at the clock, had the last word on that point after a brief submission from John Scannell on behalf of Le Mesurier.

Scannell, the last of the defence counsel, took a new line. He stated the proposition of law defining conspiracy. Once formed, a conspiracy continued in existence until it was discharged or terminated by its completion, abandonment, or frustration. 'To be in a conspiracy to murder you must be affected of the design to kill. Knowledge after the conspiracy ceased is not sufficient to make a person a party to a conspiracy. I submit, no conspiracy to murder existed after the Moors incident on

24 October 1975. Any intention to harm ceased to exist on that date. After the dog incident there was no conspiracy capable of being joined.'

His argument was simple. Allegations of Le Mesurier's attempts to contact Newton in jail, the handing-over of the money, and the telephone calls had all been in 1977. This could not make his client party to a conspiracy which had been abandoned or frustrated in 1975. The tape-recordings and the evidence of Lambert showed Le Mesurier knew – in 1977 – of a conspiracy. Lambert, his employee, had testified Le Mesurier had told him that he gave the £5000 and: '"A fool had been hired to kill Norman Scott."' But this did not amount to an admission that he had the requisite knowledge at a time before the 'dog incident', when the conspiracy was still in existence. By 1977 there had already been Newton's trial at Exeter and a TV reconstruction of the meeting at St Brides Common.

Scannell tacked on a further argument. 'Even if you felt compelled to draw the inference Mr Le Mesurier knew of a conspiracy while it still existed, that is insufficient, because knowledge without participation would not be sufficient. It was in early 1977 that Mr Le Mesurier made his physical appearance and there is no evidence of any action by him before that.'

Scannell sat down after only ten minutes, and Taylor, who was clearly looking forward to a decent lunch-break, leapt up and said he could reply quite shortly. 'I accept the proposition in law: that it is necessary to show Le Mesurier was a party while the conspiracy was still in existence,' he said. There was very clear evidence of close contact between Le Mesurier and Holmes through the evidence of Lambert and the pools-winner Gibbs, and of close contact between Le Mesurier and Deakin through the tapes. There was evidence Le Mesurier had actually paid the £5000 and then when he saw the photographer said in a panic: '"The photos will link me with Holmes."' A reasonable jury, properly directed, might conclude that somebody was not going to be used as the paymaster if they had not been privy to the conspiracy.

Anyway, there was direct evidence on the tapes which was quite sufficient to dispose of Scannell's submission. Miller and Le Mesurier had talked about 'all the arrangements that were made with Andrew [Newton] standing'. 'This must mean a jury might conclude that means Le Mesurier was one who made arrangements with Newton *before* he undertook to do what he did.'

There were several references (and here Taylor managed to slide in his reply to Mathew) to £10,000. Le Mesurier had said he was making arrangements for Newton to be paid 'Ten Gs'. So it was not a frightener. '"Ten Gs tax free ain't bad, is it?"' he had said. 'Put with the fact that he paid the money, a jury might conclude he was in the arrangement to pay £10,000 for Newton.' Le Mesurier, Taylor said, had 'an intimate and total involvement in the conspiracy'.

Scannell's one-sentence reply was lost in the sudden hubbub of relief from the press benches that the submissions were finally over.

Edward Donati leaned forward, looking grave at the burden of responsibility he and his two colleagues had to face. He explained to counsel that they had been sitting for so long and had so much to consider. He did not want to have everybody hanging round the court, so he proposed to adjourn until the next day. 'I hope we will be in a position tomorrow morning to reconvene at ten, when we might be able to give our findings.' Taylor thanked him for his consideration and Donati, clearly apprehensive he had over-committed himself, hurriedly added a warning that they might not have finished by then.

Donati rose. The press noted the time his bottom left the seat with more than usual care. It was 1.02 p.m. The journalists were running a sweepstake on how long the bench would need to retire.

The final morning was rather an anti-climax. Sir David had urged the magistrates to treat Thorpe exactly as they would an ordinary Somerset defendant. And so they did.

Mrs Griffiths had dressed up with a velvet jacket and a silk scarf. Otherwise there were no frills. Winder fussily told the four defendants to get up from their usual seats scattered round the court, and shepherded them into line in front of the dock.

Donati read out their full names, 'We find there is a *prima facie* case in respect of each of the four of you. There is also a *prima facie* case in respect of you, Thorpe, of inciting Holmes to murder Norman Scott,' he said simply. Challes wrote on his notebook: '10.09. There is a *prima facie* case.' Thorpe stood rock still and rigidly expressionless. Deakin, his salmon-pink suit clashing with his ginger hair, looked suddenly glum. Winder went through the necessary formal technicalities. They all four denied the charges. Sir David said Thorpe reserved his defence.

Donati announced formally: 'You will all be committed to stand trial.'

John Mathew got to his feet by pre-arrangement with the other lawyers, including the Crown. Normally local committals would be sent to the Crown Court at Exeter. But from a practical point of view the amenities at the Central Criminal Court (the Old Bailey) were much more suitable. It would save money and be more convenient. He added delicately that the interests of justice – 'you will understand what I mean by that' – would be best served by trying the case 'on completely neutral ground'. The Bench agreed.

Bail was continued on the same terms as before – one surety of £5000 each – but there was a new proviso. In future the defendants would have to apply through a court, not just to the police, if they wanted their passports back to go abroad. And for Thorpe there was to be an extra hour of technical custody. His surety, Lord Avebury, the former Liberal MP, Eric Lubbock, had been unable to come to court. He was in London, hurrying to Cannon Row police station in Westminster to sign the relevant form. Thorpe had to wait for the confirmatory telex to reach Minehead police.

Before the court rose, Deakin and Le Mesurier were granted legal aid for one counsel and one solicitor each. Taylor tidied up some loose ends by getting formal consent for forensic examination of three letters handwritten by Scott, and of the visitors' book from the home of Thorpe's mother, where the 21-year-old Scott claimed he had spent his first night with the young MP.

Deakin had nothing to say to the reporters clustered outside. Le Mesurier volunteered that he was going to do his garden now, instead of the endless crosswords. Holmes said briefly: 'I am going home to get ready for Christmas.' Jeremy Thorpe had nothing to add to the one sentence he had spoken in court that morning – the only words he addressed to the magistrates during the entire three and a half weeks:

'I plead not guilty and will vigorously defend this matter.'